Ransomware Revealed

A Beginner's Guide to
Protecting and Recovering from
Ransomware Attacks

Nihad A. Hassan

Apress®

Ransomware Revealed: A Beginner's Guide to Protecting and Recovering from Ransomware Attacks

Nihad A. Hassan
New York, USA

ISBN-13 (pbk): 978-1-4842-4254-4   ISBN-13 (electronic): 978-1-4842-4255-1
https://doi.org/10.1007/978-1-4842-4255-1

Managing Director, Apress Media LLC: Welmoed Spahr
Acquisitions Editor: Susan McDermott
Development Editor: Laura Berendson
Coordinating Editor: Rita Fernando

Cover designed by eStudioCalamar

Cover image designed by Pixabay

Distributed to the book trade worldwide by Springer Science+Business Media New York, 233 Spring Street, 6th Floor, New York, NY 10013. Phone 1-800-SPRINGER, fax (201) 348-4505, e-mail orders-ny@springer-sbm.com, or visit www.springeronline.com. Apress Media, LLC is a California LLC and the sole member (owner) is Springer Science + Business Media Finance Inc (SSBM Finance Inc). SSBM Finance Inc is a **Delaware** corporation.

For information on translations, please e-mail rights@apress.com, or visit www.apress.com/rights-permissions.

Apress titles may be purchased in bulk for academic, corporate, or promotional use. eBook versions and licenses are also available for most titles. For more information, reference our Print and eBook Bulk Sales web page at www.apress.com/bulk-sales.

Any source code or other supplementary material referenced by the author in this book is available to readers on GitHub via the book's product page, located at www.apress.com/9781484242544. For more detailed information, please visit www.apress.com/source-code.

Printed on acid-free paper

To my mom, Samiha, thank you for everything.
Without you, I'm nothing.

—Nihad A. Hassan

Table of Contents

About the Author

Nihad A. Hassan is an independent information security consultant, digital forensics and cybersecurity expert, online blogger, and book author. He has been actively conducting research on different areas of information security for more than a decade and has developed numerous cybersecurity education courses and technical guides. He has completed several technical security consulting engagements involving security architectures, penetration testing, computer crime investigation, and cyber open source intelligence (OSINT). Nihad has authored six books and scores of information security articles for various global publications. He also enjoys being involved in security training, education, and motivation. His current work focuses on digital forensics, antiforensics techniques, digital privacy, and cyber OSINT. He covers different information security topics and related matters on his security blog at `www.DarknessGate.com` and recently launched a dedicated site for open source intelligence resources at `www.OSINT.link`. Nihad has a bachelor of science honors degree in computer science from the University of Greenwich in the United Kingdom. Nihad can be followed on Twitter (`@DarknessGate`), and you can connect to him via LinkedIn at `https://www.linkedin.com/in/darknessgate`.

About the Technical Reviewer

Rami Hijazi has a master's degree in information technology (information security) from the University of Liverpool. He currently works at MERICLER Inc., an education and corporate training firm in Toronto, Canada. Rami is an experienced IT professional who lectures on a wide array of topics, including object-oriented programming, Java, e-commerce, agile development, database design, and data handling analysis. Rami also works as an information security consultant, where he is involved in designing encryption systems and wireless networks, detecting intrusions and tracking data breaches, and giving planning and development advice for IT departments concerning contingency planning.

Acknowledgments

I start by thanking God for giving me the gift to write and convert my ideas into something useful. Without God's blessing, I would not be able to achieve anything.

I want to thank the ladies at Apress: Susan, Rita, and Laura. I was pleased to work with you again and very much appreciate your valuable feedback and encouragement.

I also want to thank all the Apress staff who worked behind the scenes to make this book possible and ready for launch. I hope you will continue your excellent work in creating highly valued computing books. Your work is greatly appreciated.

Introduction

Ransomware is a category of malicious software that prevents users from accessing their computing device resources and/or personal data, typically by encrypting it. The data on the victim's computing device is taken hostage until the victim pays a ransom to remove the restriction.

Ransomware attacks are increasing and are now considered the most prevalent cybersecurity threats afflicting businesses today—the number of new ransomware variants has grown 30-fold since 2015 and currently accounts for roughly 40 percent of all spam messages. Attacks have increased in occurrence from one every 40 seconds to one every 14 seconds. Individuals, government, and private corporations are targets. Despite the security controls set up by organizations to protect their digital assets, ransomware is still dominating the world of security and will continue to do so in the future.

This book will teach you practically how to defend against this type of threat. You will learn the following and more:

- Understand the anatomy of ransomware and how it is used to extort money from its victims

- Understand ransomware components in simple terms

- Learn about the different types of ransomware families

- Learn about the attack vectors employed by ransomware to infect computer systems

- Learn what you should do to prevent ransomware attacks from successfully comprising your endpoint device and network

- Understand what you should do if a successful ransomware infection has taken place

- Understand how to pay the ransom and the pros and cons of paying

- See how to set up a ransomware response plan to recover from such attacks

Target Audience

The following people will benefit from this book:

- IT professionals

- Digital forensics examiners

- Incident response teams

- Red team members

- Vulnerability management teams

- Network administrators

- Server administrators

This book will also prove useful to anyone with adequate IT knowledge wanting to know how to mitigate and respond to ransomware attacks.

Summary of Contents

Here is a brief description of each chapter's contents:

- **Chapter 1, "Ransomware Overview"**: In this chapter, I introduce ransomware and differentiate it from other types of malware. I begin talking about malware types and their general components. Then I move on to talk about ransomware, its types, its primary targets, and the ransomware infection symptoms. This chapter also covers the notification requirements of ransomware attacks following the US and EU regulations.

- **Chapter 2, "Ransomware Distribution Methods"**: In this chapter, I discuss the different attack vectors employed by ransomware to infect computer systems. Obviously, phishing e-mails and exploit kits are the primary means used by cybercriminals to spread ransomware; however, there are more attack vectors that ransomware authors are using to infiltrate their targets.

- **Chapter 3, "Ransomware Families"**: As its name implies, this chapter lists the major ransomware families. A ransomware family can have more than one variant; I will talk briefly about each variant and show the preferred infection vector used by it.

- **Chapter 4, "Endpoint Defense Strategies"**: The preferred target for ransomware is an endpoint machine. Such devices tend to be less secure than servers, and securing them is key to protecting the whole enterprise network from malicious attacks. In this chapter, I teach you how to optimize your computing device to become more resistant against ransomware attacks and talk about the different methods used to lower the attack surface of cyber-attacks against endpoint devices.

- **Chapter 5, "Enterprise Defense Strategies Against Ransomware Attacks"**: In this chapter, I cover the main security elements that all organizations should consider when protecting their networks from malware attacks, focusing primarily on ransomware.

- **Chapter 6, "Security Awareness Training"**: In this chapter, I talk about the importance of having a security awareness training program and discuss what topics should be included in such a training program. This chapter also covers in some detail how to mitigate the most common threat vectors against computerized systems that exploit human errors, which means social engineering (SE) attacks.

- **Chapter 7, "Paying the Ransom"**: In this chapter, I answer the tough question, should you pay the ransom or not? I also talk about anonymous payment methods; there are different payment services employed by ransomware owners when taking ransoms from their victims, mainly cryptocurrency and prepaid gift cards.

- **Chapter 8," Ransomware Decryption Tools"**: In this chapter, I introduce you to different ransomware decryptors and suggest a manual method to recover from locking ransomware.

- **Chapter 9, "Responding to Ransomware Attacks"**: In this chapter, I discuss the main elements of a ransomware incident response plan and show how the existence of such a plan can greatly help to minimize ransomware damage and recover normal operations quickly.

Comments and Questions

To comment or ask technical questions about this book, e-mail the author at nihad@ protonmail.com. For additional references about the subject, computer security tools, tutorials, and other related matters, check out the author's blog at www.DarknessGate. com and the author's dedicated portal for open source intelligence (OSINT) resources at www.OSINT.link.

PART I

Introduction to Ransomware Threats

CHAPTER 1

Ransomware Overview

Rapid technological development has brought with it an increase in cyberattacks. Cybercrimes have become more complex and can lead to compromising thousands or even millions of devices simultaneously. Today there are various types of cybercrimes, and one of the latest—and most dreaded—is ransomware, also called *digital extortion* or *digital blackmail*.

Ransomware is a kind of malware that prevents users from accessing their computing device resources and/or personal data using various methods. Ransomware does not intend to bring any damage to the computer file system, instead leaving it functional to display the ransom note (i.e., payment instructions) on the victim's screen and to provide a way for the victim to pay the ransom. The data on the victim's computing device (whether it is a computer, server, tablet, smartphone, or Internet of Things device) becomes unusable until the device owner pays a ransom to remove the restriction.

Computing devices infected with ransomware will usually show a screen notice threatening the user that they must pay the ransom within a limited period of time; otherwise, there will be permanent data destruction. The perpetrators behind the ransomware then collect ransom money using anonymous payment methods (e.g., prepaid cash cards and cryptocurrencies like Bitcoin) to limit their monetary trail. Ransomware demands typically average between $300 to $2,000 for individual targets.

Earlier versions of ransomware used simple methods to lock user access to computing device resources/personal files such as denying access to system tools or the desktop. Modern ransomware variations use encryption to strongly lock the victim's personal files—making it unrecoverable without the associated decryption key.

As the dependence on digital technology increases, people rely more and more on their computing devices—whether it is a computer or a mobile device—to organize their work and personal lives. Valuable personal data is stored on these devices, often including corporate data that might contain trade secrets or business operations and

© Nihad A. Hassan 2019
N. A. Hassan, *Ransomware Revealed*, https://doi.org/10.1007/978-1-4842-4255-1_1

budgets available only in digital format. This shift to the information age means a successful ransomware attack against an unprotected system can have catastrophic consequences.

Ransomware is an ever-growing problem that hits individuals, the public sector, enterprises, and small to medium businesses (SMBs). Recent events have focused an intense spotlight on ransomware incidents, and ransomware threats are expected to worsen in the years to come. Cybersecurity Ventures[1] predicts that a ransomware attack will hit a business every 14 seconds by the end of 2019. The estimated damage costs of ransomware attacks will reach $11.5 billion annually in the same period. These numbers are nothing compared to the prediction offered by Cisco Systems, which indicates that ransomware attacks are growing more than 350 percent annually.[2]

This chapter covers the emergence of ransomware and briefly talks about its history, types, and what differentiates it from other malware types. Ransomware is a type of malware, so we will also explore malware types, components, and how ransomware achieves its persistence on victim machines. I'll start with a brief history of ransomware attacks and how they evolved over time to become the most threatening type of cyberattack in existence.

The History and Evolution of Ransomware

The ransomware threat has been around since the early days of the classic computer virus. Many studies show that the first documented ransomware, called AIDS Trojan (also known as the PC Cyborg virus), appeared in 1989. The perpetrator, a biologist named Joseph Popp, mailed 20,000 infected floppy disks to the attendees of the World Health Organization's AIDS Conference. The disks were labeled "Aids Information – Introductory Diskettes" and contained an interactive questionnaire used to trigger the malware after approximately 90 reboots of the victim's machine.

The AIDS Trojan ransomware worked by concealing all directories and encrypting file names located on the `C:\` drive on the victim's machine, making the Windows OS unusable. To remove the restriction, the victim had to pay $189 to a Panamanian

---

[1]Cybersecurityventures, "Global Ransomware Damage Costs Predicted To Hit $11.5 Billion By 2019" February 01, 2019. `https://cybersecurityventures.com/ransomware-damage-report-2017-part-2/`

[2]Cisco, "Cisco Cybersecurity Report Series" February 01, 2019. `https://www.cisco.com/c/en/us/products/security/security-reports.html#~stickynav=2`

post-office box. The AIDS Trojan ransomware was not sophisticated and used a simple symmetrical encryption algorithm to encrypt the victim machine's files that was relatively easy to overcome. However, it brought serious damage to different research centers around the world.

The next major step in ransomware evolution was in 1996 when two researchers wrote a paper presented at the IEEE Security & Privacy Conference (1996). This paper suggested a proof-of-concept program that used public key encryption to create malicious code to extort money from victim computers affected with this type of malware. The paper suggested the terms *cryptoviral extortion* and *cryptovirology* to name this type of cyberattack.

Note!   *Cryptovirology* is a term used to describe the science that combines cryptographic technology with malware to create malicious software.

Up to 2005, ransomware was not widely popular among cybercriminals, and no major incidents happened using this type of malware. This changed dramatically in 2005, however, when ransomware creators began to use encryption in their malicious code. In 2005, new ransomware variants emerged, such as Krotten, Archiveus, and GPCoder. GPCoder was the most noticeable one as it used 1,024-bit RSA encryption—considered strong encryption at that time—making the recovery of victim files using a brute-force technique difficult. At that time, antivirus companies responded to this emerging threat by adding the information (*signature*) of each discovered variant of ransomware into their antivirus signature list, resulting in stopping most of the ransomware attacks at that time.

In 2009, a different ransomware attack known as Vundo emerged; it was used to steal money from victims using scareware tactics (i.e., convincing victims to buy security software such as XPAntiVirus2009 by telling them that their computer was infected with a virus). This shifted the ransomware function to encrypting files and asking for a ransom ($40) to decrypt the files! Although Vundo is *polymorphic* malware—meaning that it changes its executable each time—antivirus vendors have continually added all the discovered Vundo variants into their virus database signatures to stop it.

In 2012, ransomware expanded its operation to target service providers and started using threatening tactics to extort money from its victims. For example, ransomware perpetrators targeted pornography and pirated software web sites and threatened their visitors by saying they had breached the law by viewing child pornography contents or had made a copyright infringement by downloading pirated contents. Accordingly, their personal files were locked by the local law enforcement agency, and they should pay a fine to the police to regain access to the locked computer (see Figure 1-1). The most notable ransomware that used such tactics in impersonating law enforcement agencies were Reveton and Kovter. Reveton collected its ransom using anonymous cash cards and Bitcoin cryptocurrency. Some sources estimated that Reveton acquired $44,000 per day for just a single country targeted.[3]

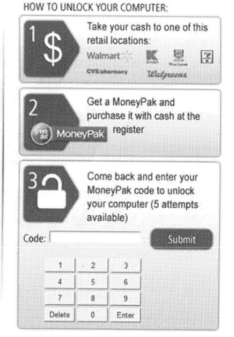

Permanent lock on

Figure 1-1.   *This ransomware infection pretends to be from a law enforcement authority.*

---

[3]Krebsonsecurity, "Inside a 'Reveton' Ransomware Operation" February 11, 2019. https://krebsonsecurity.com/2012/08/inside-a-reveton-ransomware-operation

Pushed by the success of Reveton in collecting a considerable amount of cash from its victims, different variations of ransomware began to appear in 2013 through 2015 such as Cryptolocker, Torrentlocker, Cryptowall, and Teslacrypt. These malware programs used strong encryption standards (e.g., AES and RSA-2048 bit), leading to the explosive growth in ransom payments that reached more than $325 million by late 2015.

In 2016, ransomware continued to evolve by adding more advanced features to its operations such as a countdown timer (with a ransom that increases over time if the victim did not pay) in addition to making modern ransomware variations able to propagate across computer networks automatically. Ransomware creators also added additional ways to pay the ransom and simplified the payment process, making it easy to follow by even non-computer-savvy users. Locky, Petya, and SamSam were the most notable ransomware families that appeared in that year.

Note!   Some ransomware variants like Doxware threaten to release their victim's personal data (e.g., photos, videos, confidential information, chat conversations, and trade secrets) to the public if they refuse to pay the ransom. Another variant of the Doxware ransomware is called Popcorn Time, which gives its victim the choice to either pay the ransom or infect two of their friends with it.

2016 was remarkable for the number of new ransomware families introduced. The number of ransomware families discovered in 2016 was 247—an increase of 752 percent over 2015.[4]

2017 was nominated by many security experts as the golden year of ransomware. The most notable attack was the WannaCry/WCry ransomware. This malware has spread across the globe, its ransom note supports 27 languages, and it has the ability to propagate across connected networks to infect connected servers and systems. According to Cybersecurity Ventures, ransomware attacks cost the world $5 billion in this year alone,[5] with $4 billion caused by WannaCry alone![6]

---

[4]Trendmicro, "Ransomware: Past, Present, and Future" February 11, 2019. `https://documents.trendmicro.com/assets/wp/wp-ransomware-past-present-and-future.pdf`

[5]Cybersecurityventures, "Global Ransomware Damage Costs Predicted To Hit $11.5 Billion By 2019" February 14, 2019. `https://cybersecurityventures.com/ransomware-damage-report-2017-part-2/`

[6]Cbsnews, "'WannaCry' ransomware attack losses could reach $4 billion" February 10, 2019. `https://www.cbsnews.com/news/wannacry-ransomware-attacks-wannacry-virus-losses/`

The huge increase in ransomware damage in 2017 was mainly caused after the Shadow Broker hacker group released the NSA-leaked repository of hacking tools that contains—among other tools—secret exploits that enable perpetrators to exploit vulnerabilities in Windows PCs and servers in addition to virtual private networks (VPNs) and firewall systems. Basically, the NSA-leaked tools were used by criminal groups to spread ransomware globally using unpatched vulnerabilities in Windows OS.

2018 witnessed a decline in ransomware attacks. According to reports published by Kaspersky's[7] and Malwarebytes,[8] ransomware infection fell 30 percent worldwide. Although these figures are somehow encouraging, the statistics show that while the ransomware volume declined in 2018, it became more sophisticated, and many more variants come with a self-propagation capability. Although it is difficult to foresee the future of cybersecurity exactly, Cybersecurity Ventures predicts that cybercrime damages will reach $6 trillion by 2021; the same study predicts that a ransomware attack will hit a business every 11 seconds by 2021, and the estimated damage caused by ransomware will cost the world $20 billion in 2021.[9]

Note!   Keep in mind that when we talk about ransomware damage, we are pointing to the complete loss caused by ransomware attacks. This loss includes loss of productivity, costs associated with conducting forensic investigations of affected systems and networks, the costs of restoring data from backup to resume usual operations, and the costs of hiring emergency consultants and crisis managers for enterprises.

---

[7]Kasperskycontenthub, "KSN Report: Ransomware and malicious cryptominers 2016-2018" February 14, 2019. https://media.kasperskycontenthub.com/wp-content/uploads/sites/58/2018/06/27125925/KSN-report_Ransomware-and-malicious-cryptominers_2016-2018_ENG.pdf

[8]Malwarebytes, "Cybercrime tactics and techniques: Q2 2018" February 11, 2019. https://resources.malwarebytes.com/files/2018/07/Malwarebytes_Cybercrime-Tactics-and-Techniques-Q2-2018.pdf

[9]Cybersecurityventures, "Cybercrime Damages $6 Trillion By 021" February 11, 2019. https://cybersecurityventures.com/cybercrime-damages-6-trillion-by-2021/

An example of business loss (without paying the ransom) is what happened with Atlanta's city government. In March 2018, the Atlanta government was hit by the SamSam ransomware. To rebuild its computer networks and restore its services, the city spent more than $5 million.

Now that you have a fair understanding of the ransomware history and how it has evolved to the present day, I'll briefly discuss the concept of computer malware, in general, so you can better understand the role of ransomware in this chain.

Computer Malware

Malware, short for "malicious software," is a general term used to describe all types of software programs that can bring damage or steal data from the target computing device. Most malware types need to be executed (triggered) by the user to execute their malicious code and spread to other computers and networks. Malware can spread manually (physically) using floppy disks, CD/DVDs, and USB sticks and other removable media, or they can be delivered through the Web (e.g., e-mail attachments, pirated software, free Internet programs, and social networks). They can hit different OS types (Windows, Linux, Unix, Android, iOS, and Mac). There are different classes of malware, and within each class, there are a number of subtypes. In the coming sections, I will give a high-level overview of some malware types.

Malware Types

In this section, I will classify the most known types of malware according to the type of damage caused by each one.

Viruses

This is the most classic—and oldest—term used to describe malicious computer software. The main intent of a computer virus is to bring damage to the victim's operating system files, making the system unstable and thus forcing the user to format it to return it to its original state.

Worms

The Morris worm, or Internet worm, was one of the first to be seen in the wild. In November 1988, it was distributed via the Internet and caused significant damage to the infected systems. This is another type of old-school attack that is still widely used to propagate malicious code across networks. Originally, the aim of worms was not to destroy or compromise the OS like computer viruses; instead, a worm works to spread from one machine to another through internal networks or the Internet without user intervention. Modern worms can also carry other malware, such as ransomware, to damage a host computer.

Worms usually attack e-mail clients on the victim machine (e.g., Microsoft Outlook or Thunderbird) and copy themselves to all contacts in the address book to further distribute their infection to new locations. Worms can also propagate by exploiting vulnerabilities in networking protocols. Worms can make computers run slowly because they can consume your disk space and Internet bandwidth. Worm propagations can cause a huge loss in revenue for companies when spread inside a company's intranet.

Ransomware

Ransomware is a type of malware that denies access to user files, sometimes encrypting the entire hard drive and even all the attached external hard drives and network shares, after which it demands a ransom from the user to regain access to the system and stored information. This entire book is about this type of threat.

Cryptojacking

This is a piece of code, usually written in JavaScript, that infects a computer silently when the victim clicks a malicious link in an e-mail or visits a compromised web site infected with this malware. Much cryptojacking malware is installed via exploit kits such as RIG exploit kits for Flash, Java, Silverlight, and Internet Explorer. After executing the malware, the malicious code begins working in the background to mine cryptocurrencies and then transfer the generated funds to the criminals behind it. Cryptojacking uses the same tactics employed by ransomware to infect systems.

What Is an Exploit Kit?

This is a malicious web application hosted on a compromised web site and used to automatically scan vulnerabilities on the victim machine when accessing the compromised web site to gain unauthorized access and install malware. You'll learn more about exploit kits in Chapter 2.

Scareware

Scareware, also known as *deception software* or *fraudware*, is a form of malware that uses social engineering tactics to cause shock, anxiety, or the perception of a threat in order to convince users into buying unwanted software. Scareware belongs to the digital extortion category of malicious code, similar to ransomware. For example, scareware can come in the form of a pop-up message that appears as a legitimate warning from a major antivirus vendor. The warning message will threaten a user that the computer is infected with a virus and they must purchase an antivirus software, which is fake, to clean the infection. The idea is to trick the user into purchasing something unnecessarily in order to take the user's money.

Adware

Adware (short for "advertising-supported software") delivers advertisements to the victim machine without consent. Many software creators use adware to generate revenue from their freely distributed computer programs and mobile apps. Adware bundled with free programs and apps is considered legal as long as it declares its function (e.g., displaying advertisements) clearly in the software description or the license agreement; however, the problem arises when adware comes bundled with another malicious program called *spyware* that can record and track a user's online activities in addition to stealing confidential information such as usernames and passwords.

Spyware

Spyware is a kind of tracking software similar to adware, but it is solely used for malicious intent. Spyware can monitor everything you type on your keyboard and send it to its operator. Some types install other malware (like ransomware) on the target machine to facilitate performing other malicious actions.

Trojan Horses

This is another kind of malicious software that installs silently on the victim machine. A Trojan usually comes bundled with a normal file or Internet program to trick users into downloading and installing it. A Trojan enables its operator to have full control over the infected computing device including the camera, microphone, and anything you type on your keyboard. A Trojan can also install additional malware and/or connect the infected computer to a botnet network.

Backdoors

Backdoor functionality exists within many types of malware; in simple terms, a backdoor is malicious code that opens a port on the victim machine to let the hacker (whether human or system/bot) gain unauthorized access to perform its malicious actions. As mentioned, the backdoor is incorporated into many malware types such as remote-access Trojans and Rootkits. Please note that backdoors can also come in the form of hardware embedded within the CPU, hard drives, peripheral devices, or networking equipment.

Downloaders

This is a type of malware that downloads other malware. A downloader will contain within its code a URL to download the other malware upon execution. Nemucod, which is a Trojan downloader, was used to download ransomware such as TeslaCrypt or Locky onto victim machines.

Rootkits

A rootkit is a dangerous type of malware; it has the ability to gain full access (administrative access) over the system and has the ability to prevent normal detection programs (antivirus and antirootkit programs) from noticing its presence. Some dangerous rootkits attack at the hardware level (firmware rootkits), and removal may require hardware replacement or specialized intervention.

Botnet and Distributed Denial-of-Service Attacks

A distributed denial-of-service (DDoS) is a type of cyberattack that attempts to make an online service unavailable by flooding it with traffic from multiple sources. Perpetrators build networks of infected computers, which could be millions of machines, known as *botnets*, by spreading malicious software through e-mails, web sites, and social media. Once infected, these machines can be controlled remotely by a botmaster, without their owners' knowledge, and used as an army to launch an attack against any target such as a server or a web site.

Botnets can generate huge floods of traffic to overwhelm a target. These floods can be generated in multiple ways, such as sending more connection requests than a server can handle, manipulating the TCP flags (like the well-known Christmas Tree attack did), or having computers send the victim huge amounts of random data to use up the target's bandwidth.

Other Malware Types

There are a few other types of malware that can perform similar functions to the types already mentioned.

- **Keylogger (both hardware and software)**: This is used to record victim computer activities from voice recordings, screen captures, microphones, and cameras.

- **Hack-tools**: These are simple programs used to retrieve passwords from browsers and other installed applications and can be incorporated into other malware for malicious purposes such as Mimikatz, which comes associated with the WannaCry ransomware and is used in many targeted attacks of SamSam ransomware.

Note!   Mimkatz is a hacking tool used to extract plaintext passwords, hashes, PIN codes, and Kerberos tickets from RAM. It is available at `https://github.com/gentilkiwi/mimikatz`.

- **Exploit kit**: This is a software program that takes advantage of vulnerabilities in many OSs (especially the outdated ones) and other software (especially web browsers) to force them to behave unexpectedly.

Malware Components

In general, malware is composed of the following parts:

- **Payload**: This is the actual component of the malware that causes damage to the victim machine. Examples of damage caused by malicious payload include the following:

  - Stealing confidential information such as passwords, banking information, personal files, and financial information.

  - Spying activities (e.g., monitoring victim activities on a computer).

  - Displaying unwanted ads (malicious adware) and monitoring online browsing habits to target the user with customized advertisements.

  - Adding a victim machine to a botnet network to use it later to launch DDoS attacks.

  - Modifying systems and personal files. For example, a malicious payload can delete or modify system files (e.g., bootloader), making it fail to start.

  - Downloading new malware.

  - Locking access to victim files and holding them hostage for ransom.

  - Sending spam e-mails without user consent.

  - Running a stealth background process that consumes victim machine resources (e.g., mining cryptocurrencies).

  - Giving backdoor access to a victim's machine.

Note!   These are ways a malicious payload gets executed:

- Opening an executable file (e.g., from e-mail attachments).

- Opening some types of nonexecutable files (e.g., some perpetrators embed malicious payloads within PNG files).

- Using a logic bomb to automatically execute the malicious code once some conditions are met. For example, to avoid suspicion, a disgruntled employee can instruct malware to begin executing after leaving the target company.

- **Obfuscator/packers**: The payload alone cannot do the intended damage, especially when there is a robust and up-to-date antivirus solution on the target machine. Obfuscators/packers help malware authors evade antivirus scanners and intrusion detection systems (IDSs) by changing malware code (compressing and encrypting it) to hide its malicious intent. Some software unpacks itself in memory while executing using runtime packers; this technique was originally created to compress code (make it smaller) and then decompress it in memory upon executing; however, it's now become used heavily for malicious purposes.

- **Persistence**: Malware needs to be executed through reboots to continue its work. Since Windows OS dominates the market share, the following are examples of where malware can hide in Windows to achieve its goals:

  - Startup folders

  - Autostart locations on Windows registry

  - Windows services

  - Schedule tasks

  - Temporary folders

  - Shortcut hijacking (changing the Target attribute of the shortcut icons, forcing it to download malware from malicious web sites upon launching the normal program), as shown in Figure 1-2

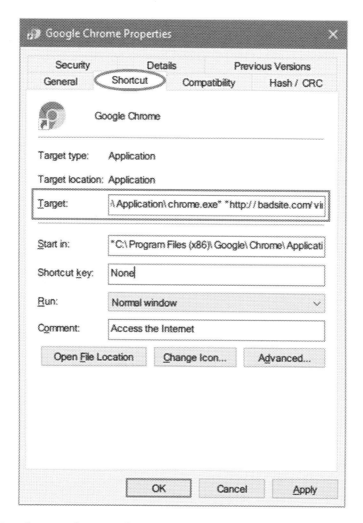

Figure 1-2. *Employing shortcut hijacking techniques to download malware upon launching the Google Chrome browser*

- **Stealth component**: Malware can achieve its stealth using different tactics such as the following:

  - Process hiding.

  - Injecting malware code into a legitimate process as a thread.

  - Sockets hiding, for example, using covert channels.

  - Hiding modules and DLL files.

- Using fileless malware such as using built-in Windows tools (e.g., PowerShell and Windows Management Instrumentation,) to execute malicious code. Detecting fileless malware is extremely difficult using traditional scanning techniques such as signature-based methods or sandboxing. The Sorebrect ransomware uses this evading technique to bypass security solutions.

- Changing the file extension. This is an old trick but is still used (e.g., `someFile.pdf.exe`).

- **Armoring**: This is a set of techniques used by malware to prevent antivirus and malware analyzers from capturing it. For example, the malware tries to detect if it is running under a virtual machine environment or a debugger or if malware analysis tools are being executed such as `tcpdump.exe` and `wireshark.exe`. The armoring technique is crucial to increase the life span of the malware and to protect its communications with the controlling servers.

- ***Command and control (C&C)***: As its name implies, the C&C center is responsible for sending instructions and other data (e.g., downloading a new version of the installed malware or distributing the encryption/decryption key in the case of ransomware attack) for malware residing on compromised machines. It is also responsible for receiving stolen data extracted from victim machines such as passwords and financial information. Some malware uses cloud-based services, such as webmail and file hosting services, as a C&C to appear as normal traffic to evade detection by security solutions.

Ransomware Types

There are mainly two types of ransomware: crypto and locker ransomware. However, ransomware belongs to the digital extortion category of cybercrime, which also contains other types of cyber crimes that aim to illicitly acquire or deny access to personal data in exchange for a monetary gain. In this section, I talk about ransomware types and list the different types of cybercrime that fall under the digital blackmail umbrella.

Note!   The end purpose of digital extortion is not always to extort money illegally through ransoms. Sometimes the end purpose is to obtain information from its victims.

Lawmakers differentiate between the *digital blackmail* and *digital extortion* terms; for instance, they consider a crime to be digital extortion when a perpetrator locks access to victim files and threatens to destroy data if the victim refuses to pay a ransom. Crimes falling into the digital blackmail category refers to the crimes that involve threatening victims, whether people or corporations, with releasing sensitive information if they refuse to cooperate.

In this book, I will use both terms interchangeably, as some variants of ransomware can do both actions.[10]

Locker Ransomware

Locker ransomware works by preventing the victim from reaching their personal files through denying access to computing resources (e.g., locking the desktop or preventing the victim from logging in) and then demanding a ransom to regain access.

Compared with crypto ransomware, typical locker ransomware types deny access to personal files using relatively simple techniques that can be overcome by any technical user; as a result, locker ransomware can be removed from the infected systems without affecting the underlying operating system and personal files.

Crypto Ransomware

This type of ransomware encrypts all personal data on the target machine, taking it hostage until the victim pays the ransom and obtains the decryption key from the attacker. Some variants of crypto ransomware will progressively delete hostage files or release them to the public if the victim fails to pay the ransom on time. Modern

---

[10]Itweb, "The reality of digital extortion" February 08, 2019. https://www.itweb.co.za/content/ G98YdqLxaoZqX2PD

ransomware families are mainly based on this type. It can have devastating effects, especially on corporate and government agencies, if no backup exists to restore operation to the state before the ransomware attack. In such cases, the victim entity has only one choice to recover the lost data, which is to pay the ransom.

After the crypto ransomware installs on the target system, it will silently search for important files (based on their extensions) and begin encrypting them; the ransomware will search for files on the local hard drive and all the attached external drives/network shares. After successfully encrypting all the computer files, the ransomware will present the user with a ransom note, showing a countdown timer and asking for payment (ransom) to regain access to hostage files. Modern crypto ransomware requests payment mostly via the Bitcoin cryptocurrency.

The majority of crypto ransomware infections will not damage the victim's operating system files and will leave it functional so the user can perform some basic functions, without the ability to access hostage data that has been encrypted.

Other Types of Digital Blackmail

Now that I have defined the two common types of ransomware, I need to talk a little bit about other digital blackmail techniques used by criminals in cyberspace to extort money from their victims. There are three types.

Scareware (Fake Antivirus and Misleading Apps)

I already talked about scareware; this type of malware works by convincing victims to purchase something online that they do not need through presenting them with false security alerts. For instance, scareware can be found in two locations.

- When a user visits a compromised web site with scareware, the infected web site will display a pop-up that appears to be a genuine message produced by the Windows OS or by a real antivirus vendor (see Figure 1-3). This pop-up will alert the visitor that their machine is infected with a virus that cannot be removed by the ordinary antivirus program, and it asks the user to purchase one online (which is fake) to solve the issue. Other variants of scareware give the visitor an option to make a free call to a technician to solve the problem remotely, where further social engineering tactics can be applied to acquire confidential information from victims.

19

- If a user sees such pop-up alerts while not browsing online, this means their machine is infected with scareware.

Figure 1-3. *Example of a scareware alert pretending to be from ZoneAlarm*

DDoS Extortion

A distributed denial-of-service can be considered a sort of digital blackmail when attackers threaten a target entity (e.g., online banks, retailers, or any organization that relies heavily on their online presence to generate revenue) and ask for money to not target them with such an attack. If cybercriminals succeed to extort money using this method, it is likely that the victim entity will not report the crime.

Data Compromise Ransom

In this type of digital extortion, a perpetrator will threaten the victim to release compromised data to the public unless a ransom is paid. Such tactics can prove effective when targeting both individuals and corporate victims.

Differences Between Ransomware and Other Malware Types

As mentioned, ransomware is a subtype of malware; however, there are many distinct characteristics that distinguish it from other malware types.

- Some malware types aim to steal user confidential information (e.g., usernames, passwords, keystrokes, and personal files) or to provide outsider access to the victim machine. More malicious malware types will bring damage (e.g., deleting files, changing system configurations, or reformatting and corrupting the underlying OS files) to the infected OS files, making it inoperable. Ransomware, on the other hand, encrypts victim machine files and announces its presence with a ransom note. The ultimate purpose of ransomware is to extort money from its victims without damaging the underlying OS or stored data.

- Ransomware does not require administrative privileges to encrypt files on the victim machine. Unlike other malware, which mostly requires admin access on the target machine, ransomware depends on the current permission assigned to the victim machine within the organization to encrypt all personal files, whether it is stored locally or on a network share, that this victim has access to.

- Encryption ransomware has the ability to encrypt all file types, in addition to its ability to scramble file names, making victims unaware of the actual number of files encrypted.

- Ransomware requests payments via anonymous payment methods, typically Bitcoin.

- Ransomware uses different evasion techniques to surpass security solutions like antivirus software and firewalls.

- Some ransomware types connect the victim machine to other networks of botnets to use it as a weapon in other cyberattacks.

- Ransomware can propagate across internal networks and through the Internet.

- Ransomware can steal sensitive information from the victim's machine and send it to its operators for blackmail purposes.

- Sophisticated ransomware is location-aware, meaning that it targets victims according to their geographical area and presents ransom notes using the target area's language.

Ransomware Symptoms

It is relatively easy to find out if you are affected by ransomware. The symptoms include the following:

- You cannot open your files; you always receive an error message that the file you are trying to access has the wrong extension (e.g., Windows asks you "How do you want to open this file?") or it is corrupted (see Figure 1-4).

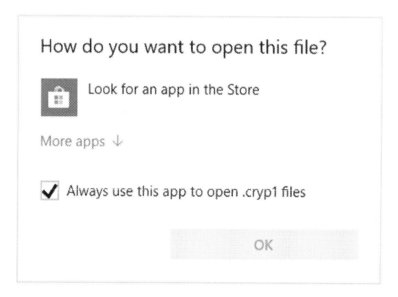

Figure 1-4. *Windows 10 dialog when the user tries to open a file with an unknown extension*

- The ransomware may change your desktop wallpaper and replace it with a ransom note.

- Your computer is locked, and you cannot access your desktop. A splash screen displaying the ransom note appears instead and covers the whole screen asking you to pay a ransom within a limited time frame; otherwise, your data will get lost forever.

- A ransom note may appear in a form of a program window that does not cover the whole screen, and the user cannot close it. A countdown timer is available within this window to alert the user about the remaining time before increasing the ransom or losing the data if the user fails to pay the ransom.

- You see instruction files in all directories that contain files encrypted by the ransomware; these files have different formats such as TXT, PNG, and HTML and the name is written in capital letters (e.g., YOUR_FILES_ARE_ENCRYPTED.HTML and YOUR_FILES_ARE_ ENCRYPTED.TXT).

- Your stored file names are scrambled and have a different extension or no extension at all.

Primary Targets of Ransomware Attacks

Before 2015, the majority of ransomware victims were individuals; however, in 2015, ransomware operators shifted their attention to target enterprises and academic organizations to acquire more guaranteed money from their attacks. In these cases, Microsoft Office and database files were the primary targets.

Enterprises are a big target of ransomware; however, anyone is subject to being a victim of such attacks such as celebrities, politicians, individuals, public and private organizations, and even charity and nonprofit organizations. Ransomware campaigns are sent in bulk (for example, sending spam e-mails with a link to download the ransomware) to infect as many devices as possible.

In 2016, the healthcare industry became a top target of ransomware attacks for many reasons. The rapid adoption of IT technology in hospitals and healthcare centers was not accompanied the necessary IT security training to combat potential cyberattacks; in addition, the health sector is particularly sensitive to any disruption of service, which makes the healthcare industry attractive to ransomware attacks.

Ransomware infects almost all IT devices types including servers, mobile devices, and many types of IoT devices in addition to storage devices attached to victim machines such as USB sticks, SD cards, digital cameras, and external hard drives (see Figure 1-5).

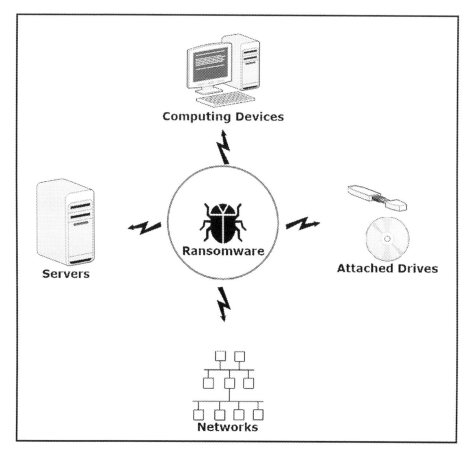

Figure 1-5. *Devices that ransomware can infect*

Most ransomware campaigns target Windows OS and Android devices because the global market share for OSs is dominated by these two operating systems, according to recent statistics published by StatCounter in January 2019 (see Figure 1-6).

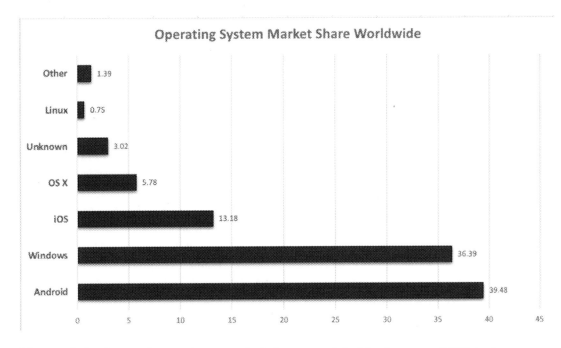

Figure 1-6. *Operating system market share worldwide, January 2018 to January 2019 (data source: http://gs.statcounter.com/os-market-share#monthly-201801-201901-bar)*

However, this does not mean that cybercriminals do not target other device types. According to Datto's report "Global State of the Channel Ransomware Report 2018," ransomware attacks on Apple OS and iOS have increased about 500 percent compared to 2017.[11] Legacy systems, especially industrial and healthcare equipment, that's still in operation and cannot receive further updates (patches) are also predicted to become a top target of ransomware attacks in the future.

To conclude, the crucial factor in determining the best target of ransomware is not the type of business or the work nature of an individual. Successful ransomware attacks rely on the type of technologies used by the victim, the level of IT knowledge, vulnerabilities existing on the victim's computing devices and connected networks, and outdated operating systems and applications that cannot receive further updates from the manufacturer, in addition to the overall cybersecurity strategy implemented by the organization.

---

[11]Datto, "Datto's Global State of the Channel Ransomware Report 2018" February 14, 2019. https://www.datto.com/blog/dattos-global-state-of-the-channel-ransomware-report-2018

Notification Requirements of Ransomware Attacks

There are legal consequences concerning any type of cyberattack that involves compromising a user's personal data. The first legal issue that we need to consider of ransomware attacks is the notification requirements.

A notification requirement depends on the jurisdiction and the industry type. For example, in the United States, all states have implemented data breach notification laws. Under these laws, the victim entity (e.g., corporations, charity organizations, educational institutes, service providers, social web sites, or any entity/web site that keeps personal information about its customers/clients) must inform the authorities of any security breach that involves accessing personally identifiable information (PII) of its users.

Note!   PII is any information that can be used alone or with other information to identify or locate a single person. It includes the following: name, Social Security number, passport number, national ID number, place of birth, gender, father and mother names, biometric records, or any other detail that uniquely belongs to you and is personally identifiable.

In the United States, the Health Insurance Portability and Accountability Act (HIPAA)[12] requires any entity suffering from a data breach that resulted in accessing patient health information (PHI) to notify the affected individuals, the Secretary of HHS (U.S. Department of Health & Human Services), and the media (for breaches affecting more than 500 individuals) in accordance with the HIPAA breach notification requirements. According to HIPAA rules, a breach is defined as "...the acquisition, access, use, or disclosure of PHI in a manner not permitted under the [HIPAA Privacy Rule] which compromises the security or privacy of the PHI."[13]

---

[12]HHS, "FACT SHEET: Ransomware and HIPAA" February 09, 2019. https://www.hhs.gov/sites/default/files/RansomwareFactSheet.pdf

[13]See also Section 13402 of the Health Information Technology for Economic and Clinical Health (HITECH) Act.

When a ransomware attack results in encrypting electronic protected health information (ePHI), a breach is considered to have occurred, because according to the HIPAA Privacy Rule, attacker encryption of data qualifies as the possession of this data, even though this data has not been seen by the attacker. In this case, the same notification rules apply as with a PHI data breach.

Note!   If the ePHI was already encrypted in accordance with the Guidance to Render Unsecured Protected Health Information Unusable, Unreadable, or Indecipherable to Unauthorized Individuals,[14] then there is no need for breach notification.

In the European Union, the General Data Protection Regulation, which was enacted to protect the privacy of EU citizens (enforced on May 25, 2018), requires companies working with EU citizens' personal data to report any data breach within 72 hours. The fines imposed for breaching this regulation are costly (4 percent of the global annual turnover, or €20 million).[15]

As the ransomware threat continues to grow and diversify, it is important for companies that collect/handle personal information of users to understand the reporting requirements of its jurisdiction in case a data breach occurs to avoid any late notification.

---

[14]HHS, "Guidance to Render Unsecured Protected Health Information Unusable, Unreadable, or Indecipherable to Unauthorized Individuals" February 11, 2019. `https://www.hhs.gov/hipaa/for-professionals/breach-notification/guidance/index.html`

[15]Morganlewis, "WannaCry Ransomware Cyberattack Raises Legal Issues" February 10, 2019. `https://www.morganlewis.com/pubs/wannacry-ransomware-cyberattack-raises-legal-issues`

Summary

Ransomware has proven to be a highly effective form of cyberattack afflicting both businesses and individuals. In this chapter, I gave a high-level definition of ransomware, its work, its types, and how it is different from other malware types. I also talked about computer malware in general and how malware achieves its persistence and stealth on the victim machine. Finally, I covered the notification requirement imposed by laws in the United States and the European Union concerning data breaches.

In the next chapter, I talk about how ransomware infects computer systems and introduce the stages of a ransomware attack.

CHAPTER 2

Ransomware Distribution Methods

Ransomware activities are escalating year after year, with more attacks noted all over the world. Seemingly no one is immune to such threats. Malware authors are continually developing new and sophisticated ransomware variants that can evade detection and employ new techniques to infect more systems.

In this chapter, I will discuss the different attack vectors employed by ransomware to invade computer systems, leaving the discussion of preventive measures until Chapter 4. Ransomware uses the same techniques used by other malware types to spread, so understanding ransomware distribution techniques will help you mitigate its risks before it invades your systems.

E-mail

E-mail is the greatest gateway used by cybercriminals to spread ransomware. Research conducted by IBM in 2017 concluded that 59 percent of ransomware attacks come via phishing e-mails, and 91 percent of all malware is delivered via e-mail systems.[1]

E-mail services can be utilized in different ways to spread ransomware (see Figure 2-1), mainly through spam and phishing e-mails, as you are going to see next.

Ransomware—and other types of malware—can utilize an e-mail service to spread by disguising itself as an e-mail attachment. When unaware users download and open the malicious attachment, ransomware will infect the system instantly.

Another technique to spread ransomware via e-mail messages is to embed links (URLs) to malicious web sites—containing ransomware—in the e-mail body. When users click such links, they are redirected to a malicious web site that in turn infects their system.

---

[1]Vadesecure, "Ransomware Statistics 2017" February 10, 2019. https://www.vadesecure.com/en/ransomware-statistics-2017/

© Nihad A. Hassan 2019

N. A. Hassan, *Ransomware Revealed*, https://doi.org/10.1007/978-1-4842-4255-1_2

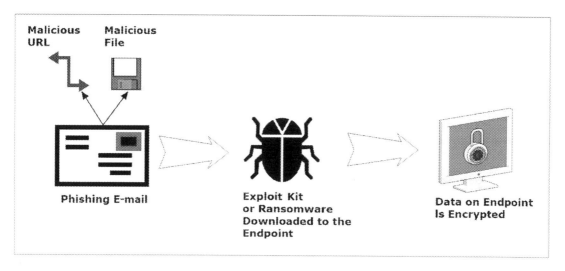

Figure 2-1. *How ransomware infects systems using e-mail messages*

E-mails used for malicious purposes are called *spam* or *phishing* e-mails. Such e-mails employ social engineering tactics to convince recipients to download/open the malicious attachment or to visit the infected sites.

Spam E-mail

Spam, also known as junk e-mail, is any unsolicited e-mail sent to a person or group of recipients through the e-mail system. Spam is commonly used in advertising campaigns for business promotions; however, it can also be used for more dangerous purposes such as spreading malware or acquiring confidential information such as login credentials and financial information from the victims. The term *unsolicited* means the recipients did not give their permission to receive such e-mails.

According to Statista, the estimated number of sent and received e-mails per day was 281 billion in 2018 and will reach 293 billion in 2019.[2] The interesting fact is that as of September 2018, spam messages accounted for 53.5 percent of e-mail traffic worldwide.[3] In other words, more than half of all e-mails worldwide are spam. Figure 2-2 shows a sample spam e-mail for tricking a victim into further communications.

---

[2]Statista, "Number of sent and received e-mails per day worldwide from 2017 to 2022 (in billions)" February 10, 2019. https://www.statista.com/statistics/456500/daily-number-of-e-mails-worldwide/

[3]Statista, https://www.statista.com/statistics/420391/spam-email-traffic-share/ February 10, 2019. https://www.statista.com/statistics/420391/spam-email-traffic-share/

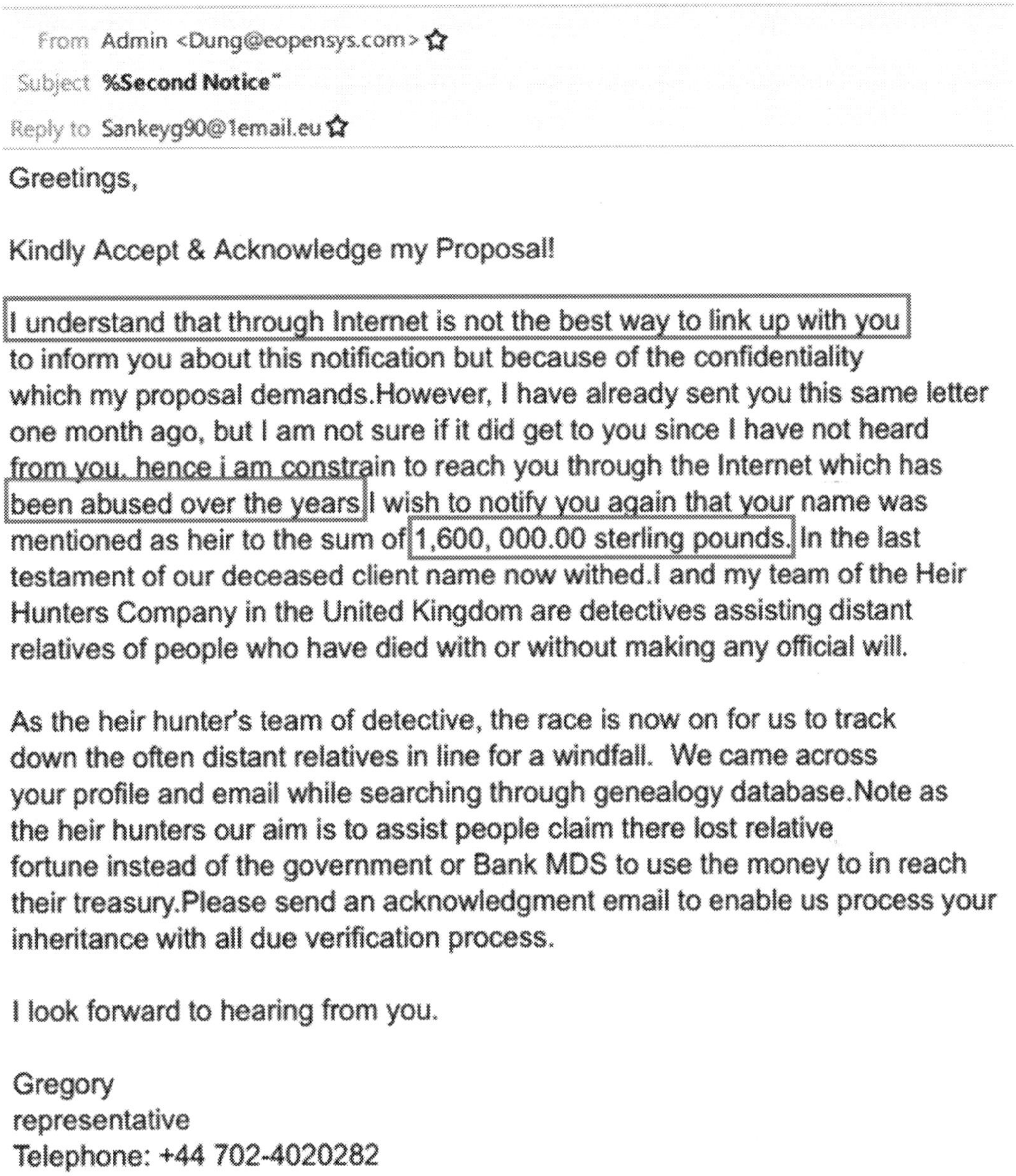

From Admin <Dung@eopensys.com> ☆

Subject %Second Notice"

Reply to Sankeyg90@1email.eu ☆

Greetings,

Kindly Accept & Acknowledge my Proposal!

I understand that through Internet is not the best way to link up with you
to inform you about this notification but because of the confidentiality
which my proposal demands.However, I have already sent you this same letter
one month ago, but I am not sure if it did get to you since I have not heard
from you, hence i am constrain to reach you through the Internet which has
been abused over the years I wish to notify you again that your name was
mentioned as heir to the sum of 1,600, 000.00 sterling pounds. In the last
testament of our deceased client name now withed.I and my team of the Heir
Hunters Company in the United Kingdom are detectives assisting distant
relatives of people who have died with or without making any official will.

As the heir hunter's team of detective, the race is now on for us to track
down the often distant relatives in line for a windfall. We came across
your profile and email while searching through genealogy database.Note as
the heir hunters our aim is to assist people claim there lost relative
fortune instead of the government or Bank MDS to use the money to in reach
their treasury.Please send an acknowledgment email to enable us process your
inheritance with all due verification process.

I look forward to hearing from you.

Gregory
representative
Telephone: +44 702-4020282

Figure 2-2. *Sample spam e-mail claiming that a recipient has unpaid money and requesting further communications. You can clearly see how the attacker tries to convince the victim to believe that the offer is true*

There are different types of spam that can be categorized according to their contents.

- **Unsolicited advertisements**: Such e-mails are sent in bulk and without the recipient's prior permission to promote goods or services from a specific commercial entity. Although laws around the world prohibit this kind of advertisement, it's still widely prevalent online.

- **Phishing scams**: In this type, spam e-mails are sent in bulk to a large number of people. A phishing e-mail (see Figure 2-3) will pretend to be genuine (from a trustworthy source) by using the same format that the legitimate company uses in its formal communications in addition to using clever wording to draw the victim's attention. Phishing aims to collect user-sensitive information (such as login information, financial and credit card information, or even personal details) by tricking a victim into handing the information to the attacker or into opening an attachment that contains malware within it.

- **Spear phishing**: Unlike phishing e-mails that are sent in bulk, spear phishing is a personalized attack that targets a specific individual, organization, or corporation to steal sensitive information or to install malware on the target user's computer.

- **Whale phishing**: This attack is similar to spear phishing and uses the same tactics, but it differs in that it is directed at high-profile employees within organizations (e.g., CEOs or CFOs) to steal sensitive information that other low-level employees do not have access to.

- **E-mail spoofing**: This is another type of phishing e-mail. Spoofed e-mails work by changing the e-mail header (the sender and e-mail ID) to look like it originated from a legitimate source. Recipients are more willing to open/download attachments from e-mails appearing coming from legitimate sources. Similar to other phishing types, spoofed e-mails can carry malicious attachments and contain malicious URLs to install malware on the victim machine.

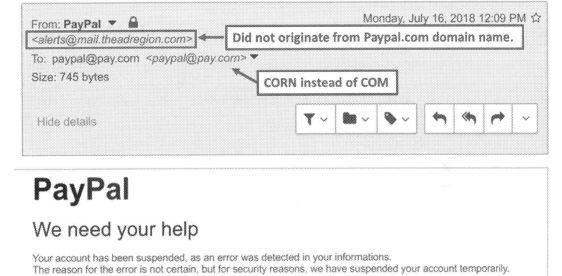

Figure 2-3. *Sample phishing e-mail to steal PayPal account information. Once a victim clicks the "Update your information" link, they will get redirected to the forged web site shown at the bottom left*

There are other types of phishing, but they all use similar tactics to convince the victim to hand over sensitive information or to install malware unintentionally.

Watering Hole Attacks

This is another type of personalized attack; it works by monitoring the target's online browsing habits so the attacker knows which web site is frequently visited by the target and then tries to infect the web site with malware. Once the victim returns to visit this web site, there is a high probability that they will get infected with the malware. Attackers select less secure and more vulnerable web sites/blogs to plant their malicious code when doing a watering hole attack.

Malvertising

Also known as malicious advertising, in this type, attackers abuse legal advertisement channels (e.g., Google Adsense) to spread malware through injecting malicious code inside ads and web pages.

Most large web sites outsource their advertisement activities to a reputable third-party vendor. The third-party vendors will in return resell some of the advertisement space, allowing other people to publish their own ads using a self-service platform. Criminals can abuse this service to spread malware.

In practice, malicious ads either can appear as a pop-up drawing user attention to click it or can be utilized to download automatically when a victim loads the web page that is hosting the malicious ad in a browser.

An example of malvertising infection can works as follows:

1. An attacker purchases ad space on legal advertisement networks and web pages.

2. An attacker conceals malicious code inside these ads.

3. When the victim loads the page holding the malicious ad, it will direct their machine to a malicious server or compromised web site hosting an exploit kit.

4. The exploit kit executes and begins evaluating the victim's machine for vulnerabilities. When a vulnerability is found, some malware is installed on the victim machine.

Exploit Kits

This is one of the fastest growing online threats. Exploit kits allow cybercriminals to obtain full control over the victim machine without their knowledge—all they need is to redirect victims to the malicious server hosting the exploit kit.

An exploit kit is a web-based compromise platform/framework that allows attackers to semi-automate exploitations by evaluating/detecting the victim's OS/application vulnerabilities and matching them to the repository of exploits stored within the exploit kit. This allows attackers to select the correct exploit for the target victim machine. Exploit kits are composed of the following parts (see Figure 2-4):

1. **Landing page**: This page contains the code responsible for assessing the victim machine for vulnerabilities. For instance, it scans the victim's web browser and installed add-ons to see whether there are any vulnerabilities that can be exploited.

2. **Gate**: The landing page transfers the victim into the second component of the exploit kit, which is the gate. The gate is a piece of code that evaluates a victim's machine to decide whether to continue the exploit or to cease it based on predefined criteria set by the attacker. For example, an attacker's predefined criteria can include the following conditions:

   - If the exploit is targeting Windows OS and the current victim is using Linux, there is no need to continue the exploit.

   - Some attackers may want to spread ransomware in a specific geographical area (e.g., United States and Canada only). If the visiting victim is from an African country, there is no need to continue the exploit.

   - Some advanced exploit kits check to see whether the victim's machine is using virtualized technology (e.g., a browser sandbox or virtual machine). In such cases, the attack will cease.

3. **Exploit**: After the gate verifies that a victim's machine is vulnerable and it is within the scope of the attack, the exploit will execute and use a vulnerable application (e.g., Adobe Flash, the Java Runtime Environment, or Microsoft Silverlight) or an unpatched OS to run malware on the victim's machine.

4. **Payload**: After successfully exploiting the vulnerable application on the victim's machine, the exploit kit will send a payload to do the real damage. The payload can be any type of malware or simply a downloader that downloads other malware on the victim's machine.

Now that you understand how an exploit kit works, you need to know how victims are directed to the landing page. Victims can be redirected to the landing page of the exploit kit using different methods. For example, criminals spread their malicious code via advertisements (malvertising) or by injecting the malicious URL into legitimate web sites like news and shopping sites. Once a user visits a compromised web site and loads its contents, the user will silently get redirected to the landing page of the exploit kit, resulting in triggering the attack automatically.

Many criminal groups operating on the Darknet offer their exploit kits for rent on a monthly basis, rising a new infection vector in the cybersecurity world called *exploit kit as a service*.

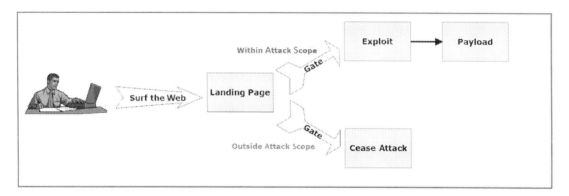

Figure 2-4. *How an exploit kit works and its components*

The most well-known exploit kits currently in use are Angler, RIG-v EK, Fallout EK, Magnitude, and Neutrino.

USB and Removable Media

Cybercriminals are still using USB devices to launch attacks against computerized systems. Although USB device–based attacks fall under local threats—they require the attacker to have physical access to the target machine unlike other types of cyberattacks that target computers via the Internet—they have still increased dramatically over the years because of a lack of cybersecurity awareness of end users.

There are many types of malware—especially worms—that spread via USB sticks and removable media. Once a victim inserts the compromised USB stick into a machine, the malware on it will install automatically. Some malware types—like ransomware and worms—can propagate and infect all computers connected to the same network.

Malicious actors use different methods to infect and spread malware via USB drives. For example, some attackers intentionally drop USB drives loaded with malware in the target organization's parking lot, hoping that one of the employees will insert one of the infected USBs into their work machine. An example of malicious ransomware spread via USB drives is the Spora ransomware.

Note!   An experiment conducted by the University of Illinois to measure the effectiveness of a USB-based attack concluded with worrying results. Experimenters from this university dropped 297 unlabeled USB flash drives around the university campus. The majority of devices were picked up by university employees and students (98 percent), and half of them were inserted into university work computers.[4]

A famous cyberattack conducted via USB drive was the Stuxnet worm in 2010. This attack resulted in installing malware on an Iranian nuclear facility network.

Pirated Content Web Sites

Malware can come bundled with other software programs, especially those downloaded from the Internet. The infection happens when you install an infected program on your machine and the malware within it installs itself—silently—onto your computer at the same time.

Some computer users do not have enough money to purchase a license for commercial software, so they opt to illegally download pirated software from the Internet to save costs.

Programs downloaded from web sites hosting pirated content (e.g., Torrent web sites) come associated with an executable program named Crack, Patch, or keygens to unlock the pirated program trial version, making it work like the paid one. Running executable programs to unlock legitimate software is dangerous, especially because the pirated program instructs the user to turn off antivirus software to avoid any conflicts while installing. Most Crack, Patch, and keygen executables will disguise malware, which will install silently upon execution.

---

[4]Elie, "Users really do plug in usb drives they find" February 10, 2019. `https://elie.net/publication/users-really-do-plug-in-usb-drives-they-find/`

Microsoft Office Macros

Microsoft Office macros are a set of instructions and commands (consider them like mini-computer programs) written using Visual Basic for Application (VBA) for automating repetitive tasks in Microsoft Office suite programs such as Excel and Word.

Microsoft Office macros have been exploited by malicious actors to do malicious actions (e.g., using the VBA KILL command to delete files) or to install malware on victim machines. Basically, cybercriminals distribute Microsoft Office files online with a malicious macro embedded within them, and when a user opens an infected file, the macro performs its malicious actions on the victim's machine.

Older versions of Microsoft Office have the macro feature enabled by default. However, this poses a major security risk. Beginning with Office 2003, Microsoft added a macro security level preventing macros from loading automatically (see Figure 2-5).

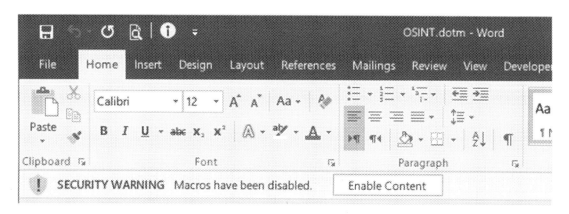

Figure 2-5. *Sample warning message issued by Microsoft Word 2016 upon opening a file with macro content*

An example of ransomware that infects machines using the macro feature via a Microsoft Word document is the Locky ransomware.

Ransomware as a Service

Businesses are shifting their operations from locally installed OSs and applications to software packages that run in the cloud. There are different models adopted by businesses to achieve this. The following are the three most common ones:

- **Software as a service (SaaS)**: Accessing and using applications hosted in the cloud via the Internet. Examples include Google Apps for Education and Microsoft Office 365.

- **Infrastructure as a service (IaaS)**: Using remote IT infrastructure instead of purchasing in-house equipment. Examples include Amazon Web Services and Google Computer Engine.

- **Platform as a service (PaaS)**: Typically used by developers to develop applications in the cloud.

Ransomware as a service (RaaS) adopts a similar approach to SaaS but on the malicious side. RaaS is an online software package sold in underground markets and/or forums using a subscription-based model. It aims to simplify ransomware attacks for novice cybercriminals in exchange for a cut of the ransom payments acquired by the RaaS agents.

RaaS is a dangerous emerging model that usually involves three actors: a malware author, a service provider, and agents (attackers). Malware authors develop ransomware code, integrate it into an online dashboard, and present it for sale or rent. They also provide step-by-step instructions on how to launch ransomware attacks so criminals with no technical background can use this service easily.

Cybercriminals access the RaaS dashboard where they can create a new ransomware attack, check the status of already launched attacks, and monitor payments from their successful attacks. Most RaaS adopts a profit-sharing model, where the final income—generated from ransom payments—is divided among the ransomware coders (authors), the service providers (the ones hosting the RaaS), and the affiliated cybercriminals.

Figure 2-6 shows a sample RaaS provider called DataKeeper, where attackers can customize the payload before downloading the final ransomware file. This service is hosted on the TOR network; accessing it requires using the TOR Browser (`https://www.torproject.org/download/download.html`).

39

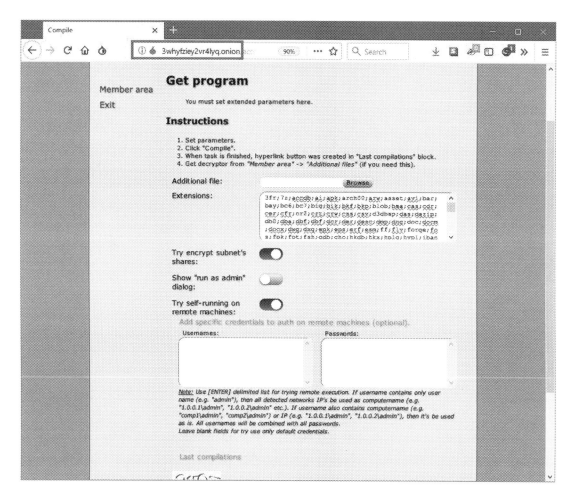

Figure 2-6. *DataKeeper RaaS compilation page used to create the ransomware*

Remote Desktop Connection

With the explosive growth of Internet communications worldwide, many companies outsource their IT support to third-party companies. These contractors can be in the same country or overseas.

To enable these contractors to perform their job of monitoring and troubleshooting Windows networks, Windows offers a built-in feature (also available for other OSs) called Remote Desktop Protocol (RDP) that allows a user to mirror the screen, keyboard, and mouse of a remote system on the local device (see Figure 2-7). RDP uses port 3389 to communicate.

Attackers can utilize brute force (by exploiting weak passwords) and social engineering techniques to acquire RDP login credentials. After acquiring this information, the path becomes open to the victim's computer and network. Perpetrators can install any type of malware (e.g., deploying ransomware) on the victim's machine in addition to infiltrating the target network.

Note!   In a brute-force attack, the attacker tries all possible combinations to find the correct password/key.

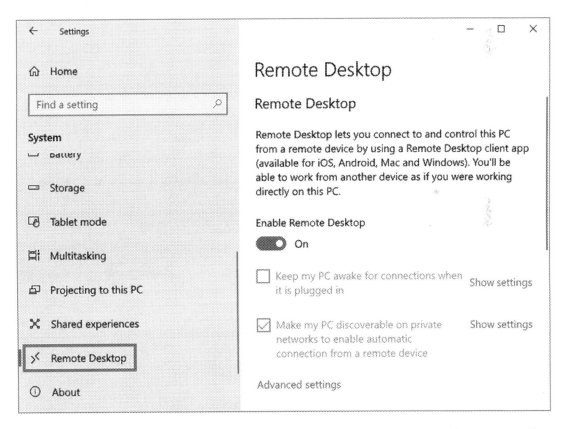

Figure 2-7. *Enable/disable RDP by going to Settings and then System (Windows 10)*

Warning!   Shodan (`https://www.shodan.io`), a search engine for locating Internet of Things (IoT) devices, can be used to locate exposed RDP clients.

Note!   Cybercriminals are selling backdoors and compromised RDP accounts for just $10 each. This market is very active—and growing—on the Dark Web.

Managed Service Providers

A *managed service provider* (MSP) is an IT service provider that delivers various IT services such as remote support for IT infrastructure, network monitoring, remote firewall and intrusion detection system (IDS) administration, mobile device management, security incident and breach investigation, and other consulting services to its customers. MSP customers are usually small and medium-sized enterprises that have a small staff and need to outsource some of their IT tasks to reduce expenses. An MSP is offered on a subscription model (e.g., monthly, semiyearly, and so on).

To do their remote work, MSP providers need to use specialized software—similar to RDP in Windows—to remotely access their client's IT infrastructure. Ransomware operators have taken note of this service model and begun developing methods to hack the MSP service to distribute their ransomware (and other malware) and install it on all target MSP clients.

The GandCrab ransomware family is known to spread using this method. In the future, you can expect to see more criminal groups selecting this method to distribute their malicious code.

Botnets

I already talked about botnets in Chapter 1; a *botnet* is a compromised machine controlled by a command-and-control (C&C) server and used to launch—with other thousands or even millions of compromised machines—DDoS attacks. For instance, botnets can be exploited to play another malicious role, which is downloading ransomware or any type of malware from its C&C server to infect the computer hosting it (see Figure 2-8).

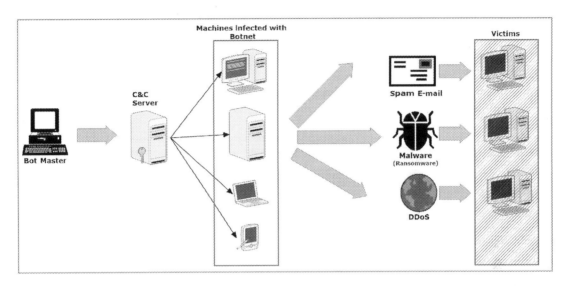

Figure 2-8. *Machines infected with botnets can be used to spread or to infect themselves with ransomware*

Zero-Day Vulnerability

Zero-day vulnerabilities are those that have not been discovered by vendors or antivirus software yet. These are vulnerabilities discovered by black-hat hackers and usually found in web browsers, browser add-ons, or applications. Sometimes they can exist on the OS itself. Criminals exploit such vulnerabilities to do their evil work (e.g., infecting computers with ransomware) without the fear of having their attacks stopped by antivirus and other security solutions. Even one hour is enough time for malicious actors to invade systems with malware.

Lack of Training

Cybersecurity attacks are making international media headlines with no sign of slowing down. Each year many high-profile organizations suffer from data breaches resulting in exposing millions of records. Different statistics and research find that a lack of security awareness (and lack of skilled personnel) plays a key role in exposing organizations to different cyberthreats, especially ransomware.

Employee awareness of IT security is considered the first line of defense in protecting information systems. Security awareness training ensures that employees are aware of the different attack techniques that may be employed by cybercriminals to break into the organization's systems and that they know how to mitigate and report such incidences to the appropriate person. For instance, no matter the types and number of security solutions (e.g., firewall and IDS) implemented to secure a specific organization's network, if an unaware employee clicks a malicious link within a phishing e-mail, it will jeopardize the entire network, making all the protective measures implemented by organization security team useless!

In Chapter 6, we will discuss in some detail the different angles of cybersecurity awareness training that need to be understood by any computer user to defend against cyberattacks.

Stages of a Ransomware Attack

There are five main stages of ransomware attack from the time it gets installed on the victim machine until it announces its presence on the victim's screen. Understanding how ransomware infects systems helps you avoid its risks.

- **Exploitation and infection:** Ransomware is introduced to the victim system through a phishing e-mail, exploit kit, or any of the means already described.

- **Delivery and execution**: If the exploitation was successful, the actual ransomware is installed on the victim machine.

- **Backup destruction**: The ransomware now searches for backup files on the victim machine and sometimes on all the attached backup storage across the network and destroys it so the victim cannot recover their system to its previous state before the ransomware attack.

- **File encryption**: Now that the ransomware has successfully destroyed the victim's backup files, it will begin encrypting the victim's files. The ransomware will establish a secure connection with its C&C server to create an encryption key pair of that machine. Please note that some ransomware can do this offline without contacting a C&C server.

- **Victim notification and extortion**: The ransomware displays the ransom note on the victim's machine and demands a payment within a specific period of time, usually three days. If the victim refuses to pay, the ransom payment may increase (this depends on the ransomware family) and lead to the complete destruction of the hostage data if no payment is made.

Why Can't Antivirus Software Detect Ransomware?

Ransomware authors always try to keep themselves one step ahead of malware defenders by employing various modern tactics to make their malicious programs undetectable by security solutions such as antivirus software, firewalls, and intrusion detection systems. For instance, ransomware is difficult to catch for many reasons.

- It uses anonymizing networks like the TOR network to communicate with the C&C servers. This connection is also encrypted to prevent security solutions from detecting it when analyzing network traffic.

- It uses a domain shadowing technique to mask the communications between the ransomware and its associated C&C servers. *Domain shadowing* refers to attackers gaining unauthorized access to legitimate domain name accounts and then creating multiple subdomains of the legitimate one and using them to pass their malicious traffic between ransomware and associated C&C servers or to direct victims to the landing page of their exploit kits.

- Ransomware can detect a victim machine to check if it is running on a real computer or in a sandbox or virtual machine; in the latter case, the ransomware attack may cease.

- The ransomware payload comes encrypted, making detecting it by antivirus programs difficult.

- Some ransomware variants employ a polymorphic model to change their malicious code, making detecting them by traditional antivirus software that use signature-based methodology infeasible.

- Ransomware can stay inactive for a long time on the victim machine waiting for some conditions to happen (e.g., until finding a vulnerable application to exploit) to start its invasion.

Note!   A study conducted by Malwarebytes found that traditional antivirus programs failed to protect about 40 percent of users who are using two or more antivirus solutions from all malware attacks.[5] Malwarebytes also released a real-time map showing traditional antivirus weaknesses in detecting malware around the globe. This map can be found at `https://www.malwarebytes.com/remediationmap/`.

Summary

Ransomware can spread using different methods, mainly by using the e-mail system or compromised web sites housing exploit kits. In this chapter, I discussed these methods and gave examples of each one. Keep in mind that many ransomware variants and other malware types have self-propagation capabilities; hence, they can identify and infect all computers connected to the victim network.

Now that you have a fair understanding about the nature of ransomware and what methods it uses to infect computer systems, we'll talk about the most famous ransomware families and cover attack techniques employed by each family to compromise their targets.

---

[5]Prnewswire, "New Research: Traditional Antivirus Failed to Protect Nearly 40 Percent of Users Using Two or More AV Solutions from All Malware Attacks" February 10, 2019. `https://www.prnewswire.com/news-releases/new-research-traditional-antivirus-failed-to-protect-nearly-40-percent-of-users-using-two-or-more-av-solutions-from-all-malware-attacks-300543625.html`

CHAPTER 3

Ransomware Families

The Most Prominent Ransomware Strains

Ransomware can be classified into groups using different criteria, for example, according to its function such as whether it is a locker or encryption ransomware. Security experts prefer to classify ransomware into families according to its code signature, which contains the sequence of commands and instructions responsible for the malicious action. For this chapter, I will mention the most prominent ransomware families and their popular variants according to their release date and talk a little bit about each one; later in the book, I will give decryption utilities for each family where available.

Ryuk

Ryuk is a crypto ransomware specialized in targeted attacks against enterprises that can afford to pay its relatively big Bitcoin ransom (15 BTC to 50 BTC). First appearing in August 2018, Ryuk is connected to the APT Lazarus hacking group, which is associated with the North Korean army. After dissimilating its source code, security researchers at Checkpoint found that Ryuk shares many similarities with the Hermes ransomware strain[1] (both use a similar encryption routine) that was first discovered in February 2017 and that uses spam campaigns and exploit kits to infect its victims.

---

[1]Checkpoint, "Ryuk Ransomware: A Targeted Campaign Break-Down" July 28, 2019, https://research.checkpoint.com/ryuk-ransomware-targeted-campaign-break

© Nihad A. Hassan 2019
N. A. Hassan, *Ransomware Revealed*, https://doi.org/10.1007/978-1-4842-4255-1_3

In two months after its initial release, Ryuk had acquired $640,000 of ransom from businesses around the world; after five months, the number had increased to $3.7 million in Bitcoin.[2] The perpetrators behind Ryuk use a unique Bitcoin address for each victim and split the received ransom money between different Bitcoin accounts before laundering the money using different Bitcoin laundering services to make tracking the ransom money almost impossible by law enforcement.

Ryuk is used mainly for tailored attacks, where attackers need to collect technical information about the target IT infrastructure before launching their ransomware attack. Unlike most ransomware strains, Ryuk needs admin privileges to execute on the target computer. Many reported attacks using this ransomware have worked by exploiting the insufficiently protected Remote Desktop Protocol (RDP) or by spear phishing to gain entry into an enterprise network. Ryuk can propagate across the infected network to infect all connected machines such as computers, data centers, network drives, and other storage devices.

Ryuk has two versions for 32-bit and 64-bit systems, and it uses AES-256 and RSA-4096 to encrypt victim files. Once executed on the victim computer, it will delete all Windows Shadow Copy copies, making the recovery of files impossible with external clean backup. Ryuk drops different versions of a ransom note (see Figure 3-1) on the victim's desktop and all the other folders where data is encrypted.

---

[2]Thenextweb, "Ryuk ransomware earns hackers $3.7M in Bitcoin over 5 months" July 28, 2019 https://thenextweb.com/hardfork/2019/01/14/ryuk-bitcoin-ransomware

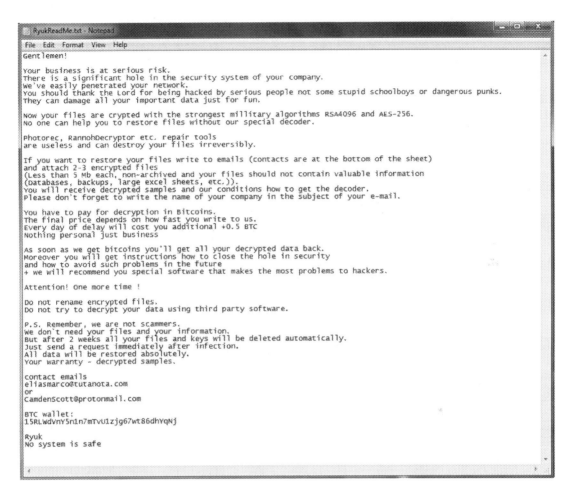

Figure 3-1. *Sample Ryuk ransom note*

Ryuk is still an active threat as of this writing; according to the Federal Bureau of Investigation (FBI), Ryuk successfully launched more than 100 attacks against U.S. businesses operating in different industries, such as logistics, technology, and healthcare, between August 2018 and mid-May 2019.[3]

---

[3]Securityintelligence, "More Than 100 US Businesses Affected by Ryuk Ransomware Since August 2018, Finds FBI" July 28, 2019 https://securityintelligence.com/news/more-than-100-us-businesses-affected-by-ryuk-ransomware-since-august-2018-finds-fbi

WannaCry

WannaCry (also known as Wcry, WNCry, WanaCrypt0r, and Wana Decrypt0r) is crypto ransomware that has worm-like capabilities. It targets computers running the Windows OS and demands a $300 ransom in the Bitcoin cryptocurrency to decrypt the data (see Figure 3-2). The ransomware operators threaten to double the ransom if it isn't paid within three days; failing to pay the ransom within one week will lead to the permanent destruction of infected files. First discovered in February 2017, it did gain international recognition until the release of the second version on May 12, 2017, when a huge campaign hit scores of countries targeting different sectors from health to telecommunications. WannaCry spreads by exploiting a Windows Server Message Block (SMB) vulnerability that provides unrestricted access to any computer running Windows. WannaCry is also able to propagate between corporate LANs automatically.

Figure 3-2. *WannaCry ransomware attack notice*

The attack—which is still considered one of the most devastating ransomware attacks ever—has affected more than 230,000 computers in 150 countries and cost nearly $4 billion in financial losses. Many countries including the United States, the United Kingdom, and Australia have confirmed that North Korea is behind this ransomware attack.

How Did WannaCry Spread?

In April 2017, the hacking group named Shadow Brokers (TSB) released various stolen hacking tools and exploits developed by the National Security Agency (NSA) to target Windows, firewalls, and IDS systems in addition to different antivirus products. WannaCry takes advantages of critical vulnerabilities discovered using these exploits.

For example, EternalBlue, which is an exploit kit developed by the NSA and released by the TSB group, allows cybercriminals to spread WannaCry by executing arbitrary code via the SMB protocol vulnerability in different Windows versions like Microsoft Windows Vista SP2, Windows 7 SP1, Windows Server 2008 SP2 and R2 SP1, Windows 8.1, Windows Server 2012 Gold and R2, Windows RT 8.1, and Windows 10 Gold 1511, and 1607, and Windows Server 2016. Once a victim opens the malicious file (e.g., opening an e-mail attachment) containing the ransomware code, WannaCry will begin propagating across all the connected LANs and to other computers across the Internet, affecting all Windows computers suffering from this vulnerability. WannaCry uses port 445 on the victim machine to install itself and infect new computers; its C&C server is located on the TOR network. Upon infecting a victim computer, WannaCry appends the .WNCRY extension to all infected files, deletes Windows Shadow Copy files, and disables Windows startup recovery to prevent any recovery of infected files. In every folder containing encrypted files, WannaCry will leave the following files instructing the victim how to behave in order to restore their files: `Please_Read_Me@.txt`, `@WanaDecryptor@.exe.lnk`, `!WannaDecryptor!.exe.lnk`, and `!Please Read Me!.txt`.

Volume Shadow Copy Service (VSS)

In Windows XP, Microsoft introduced VSS, which is an application that coordinates the creation of a consistent snapshot of computer files or volumes at a specific point in time for each partition where it is activated. This allows Windows to recover if some of its files get corrupted for any reason.

To close this vulnerability, Microsoft released a hotfix update that can be downloaded from `https://technet.microsoft.com/en-us/library/security/MS17-010`.

Cerber

Cerber is crypto ransomware that targets the Windows OS; it is widely known to be distributed via the ransomware-as-a-service (RaaS) model where developers take 40 percent of the acquired ransom profit as a fee from their affiliated criminals. It is considered one of the most prominent early adopters of the RaaS model. First appearing in 2016, Cerber infects computers using common attack vectors such as phishing e-mails and exploit kits (RIG EK, RIG-v, Nuclear Exploit Kit), and it comes bundled with free online software; however, Cerber mainly utilizes malicious Microsoft Office files with macros to spread. Cerber uses social engineering tactics to convince the victim to enable macros; for example, the opened document might not display correctly, so a message appears within it asking the victim to enable macros to view it properly (see Figure 3-3). Once a victim opens a malicious Microsoft Office document and enables macros, the ransomware begins encrypting victim files using the RC4 and RSA algorithms and changes the infected files' extensions to `.cerber`. (Modern versions of Cerber change the infected file extension to `.cerber2`, `.cerber3`, or four random characters.) Finally, after successful encryption of the victim machine, Cerber displays its ransom note as the desktop wallpaper (see Figure 3-4) and gives seven days for the victim to pay the ransom (about $500 payable in Bitcoin cryptocurrency); otherwise, the ransom amount will double. Instructions on how to pay the ransom can be found on victim desktop and in every folder the ransomware has encrypted (see Figure 3-5). Cerber has the ability to work offline, meaning that disconnecting the infected machine from the Internet will not stop the encryption routine.

Figure 3-3. *Malicious Microsoft Word document using social engineering tactics to convince users to enable macros*

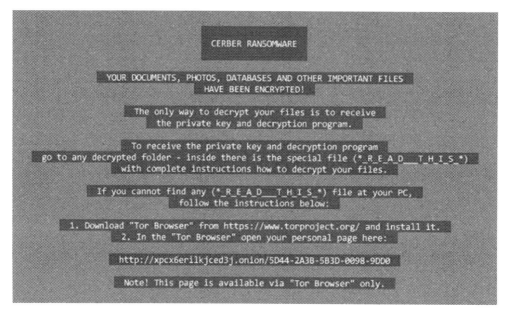

Figure 3-4. *Cerber ransomware notice*

CERBER RANSOMWARE

~ ~ ~ ~ ~

YOUR DOCUMENTS, PHOT0S, DATABASES AND OTHER IMPORTANT FILES HAVE BEEN ENCRYPTED!

~ ~ ~ ~ ~

The only way to decrypt y0ur files is to receive the private key and decryption program.

To receive the private key and decryption program go to any decrypted folder, inside there is the special file (*_READ_THIS_FILE_*) with complete instructions how to decrypt your files.

If you cannot find any (*_READ_THIS_FILE_*) file at your PC, follow the instructions below:

~ ~ ~ ~ ~

1. Download "Tor Browser" from https://www.torproject.org/ and install it.

2. In the "Tor Browser" open your personal page here:

http://▮▮▮▮hpz2n7nvgr.onion/5A1D-34BF-6B91-▮▮▮▮-▮▮▮▮

Note! This page is available via "Tor Browser" only.

Figure 3-5. *Cerbrer ransom payment notice*

There are more than six variants of the Cerber ransomware. Upon its first launch in July 2016, more than 150,000 Windows computers were infected worldwide; at the end of 2016, the criminals behind Cerber had acquired $2.3 million from ransom payments. Unlike other types of ransomware, the Cerber developers released an update for their ransomware every 8.4 days on average, adding more features to evade detection by security solutions.

Locky

First appearing in 2016, Locky targets Windows-based machines and comes supplied with anti-analysis and anti-sandboxing capabilities. This ransomware has the ability to encrypt 160 file types including source code files and databases, posing a real threat against enterprises and small businesses alike. Locky uses an RSA-2048 + AES-128 cipher to encrypt victim files on all types of storage such as local hard drives, removable hard drives, and accessible network shares. Locky generates its encryption keys on the server side and keeps each victim machine's private key there, making decrypting victim files impossible without the private key.

Note!   A variation of Locky can encrypt victim files offline without communicating with its C&C server. (See `https://blog.avira.com/locky-goes-offline/`.)

The most common technique used by Locky to infect systems is through receiving an e-mail (masquerading as order receipts, ISP complaint notices, or Dropbox account verifications) with a malicious Microsoft Word attachment; once opened by the victim, it will prompt them to enable macros because the text is not readable. Once the victim enables macros, the macro code will download the malicious code in the form of a downloader and store it in the `%Temp%` folder before executing it. After that, Locky launches and starts encrypting victim files, including the Bitcoin wallet file, along with their names and all the network share files that a victim has access to. The Locky damage does not stop here, as it scans and infects all connected devices (servers, computers, network drives) accessible to the victim across the infected network whether they are running Windows, Linux, or macOS. Locky changes the infected files' extensions to `.locky`, `.zepto`, `.thor`, `.asasin`, `.aesir`, `.ykcol`, and other extensions according to the variant. Locky also deletes Windows Volume Shadow Copy files to prevent any file recovery. Once finished, it will display a ransom notice on the victim desktop asking for a ransom between 0.5 and 1 Bitcoin (worth of $400 at that time).

A variant of Locky ransomware spread via Facebook's instant messaging. The infection occurred by using an SVG image file, which is known to allow dynamic content. A JavaScript code is hidden within the malicious image; once clicked by the target, it will direct the target to the malicious web site hosting the malicious code or an exploit kit.

There is a high probability that the criminal group behind Locky comes from Russia, as this ransomware will not execute its attack on machines located in Russia or that have the Russian language pack installed.

Petya

First appearing in 2016, Petya has mainly two variants. The first variant appeared in 2016, and the second modern one appeared in 2017, which was called NotPetya. The 2017 variant is very dangerous as it has irreversible effects and can propagate without human intervention. In addition, the NotPetya encryption keys are generated randomly and then destroyed, making data recovery impossible (it has a similar effect to hard drive wiping tools).

Petya targets the Windows OS and infects the master boot record (MBR); then it overwrites the original Windows boot loader with a malicious one and performs a restart. Then it executes its payload and begins encrypting the master file table (MFT) of the NTFS file system, making Windows unable to locate the stored files. On the next restart, Petya prevents Windows from booting and displays a ransom note instead, asking for $300 worth of Bitcoin cryptocurrency to regain access to the compromised system.

What Is the Master File Table?

Each Windows NTFS partition contains one MFT file that handles the location of files on the partition. The MFT file contains at least one record (entry) for each file stored within the NTFS partition. This record holds important information about the subject file, including its size, permission, timestamp attributes, and data contents.

Similar to other families of ransomware, Petya spreads via spam e-mails; it is also offered as an affiliate program using the ransomware-as-a-service (RaaS) model. The first version of Petya requires administrative access to a victim machine to operate; however, other variants of the first version of Petya install another ransomware called Mischa if they fail to obtain administrative privileges. The Mischa ransomware encrypts everything on the victim machine including .exe files, preventing a victim from running any programs on the infected machine. For each folder containing encrypted files, Mischa will create two ransom notes named YOUR_FILES_ARE_ENCRYPTED.HTML and YOUR_FILES_ARE_ENCRYPTED.TXT. At that time (2016), Mischa asked for 1.93 Bitcoins, which was equivalent to $850. This was a high ransom amount compared with other ransom families. As with most ransomware families, the Mischa ransomware payment site is hosted as a TOR hidden service.

NotPetya propagated using the EternalBlue and EternalRomance exploits stolen from the NSA arsenal of hacking tools. Its first attack took place in June 2017 targeting major organizations in Russia and Ukraine. However, most damage took place in the Ukraine, making security experts believe that this attack was a state-sponsored Russian cyberattack.

Although it has many commonalities with Petya and behaves in general as ransomware, NotPetya distinguishes itself through its intentional damage and ability to self-propagate. Security experts discovered after analyzing its source code that NotPetya was created to destroy data, and its ultimate goal was not to generate profits from ransoms; instead, it wants to sabotage and destroy data stored on target systems. This fact makes many security experts classify it as a "cyberweapon."

Note! The PetrWrap ransomware is an "unauthorized" version of the Petya ransomware developed by the unknown hacker group. Although it uses much of the Petya code, it adds some new commands to operate independently from the criminal group behind Petya, which is known as Janus Secretary.

SamSam

SamSam ransomware, also known as Samas, Kazi, or RDN/Ransom, is encryption ransomware used in targeted attacks. Hence, it is used to target a specific organization after conducting some form of reconnaissance against its IT systems. The criminals behind SamSam begin their intrusion by using various hacking tools, exploit kits, and brute-force techniques on a victim computer (usually the internet-facing server of the target organization). After that, they leverage legitimate tools from Windows Sysinternals (`https://docs.microsoft.com/en-us/sysinternals`), networking admin tools, and other password harvesting tools such as Mimikatz (`https://github.com/gentilkiwi/mimikatz`) to scan vulnerable devices and to gain access to the target organization network. After they have a plan to target the organization's networking and vulnerable systems, SamSam is deployed onto the first infected machine and then propagates across the infected network to encrypt all connected computers, servers, and network drives.

SamSam's first recorded attacks took place in 2016 (some sources mention it beginning in late 2015), and it continued into 2017 after increasing the ransom amount. In 2018, SamSam returned to hit high-profile targets, mainly against U.S. enterprises (e.g, Hancock Health[4]) and large public-sector organizations (e.g., the city of Atlanta[5], and the Colorado Department of Transportation[6]). It is thought that many private-sector organizations remained quiet about SamSam attacks to avoid damaging their reputations.

Unlike most ransomware families, SamSam does not use social engineering tactics such as spam e-mails and phishing to spread. Instead, it targets vulnerabilities in server applications (e.g., mainly JBoss and FTP servers) and tries to brute-force weak passwords of Remote Desktop Protocol (RDP) accounts to gain access to corporate networks. Compared with other ransomware families, SamSam needs sophisticated hacking skills by its operators as this attack needs to be carried out manually with direct supervision by its operator. Even if a victim chooses to pay the ransom, they need to run the decryptor offered by the attacker manually on each affected machine locally to restore files to their original status.

---

[4]Greenfieldreporter, "Hospital pays $55,000 ransom; no patient data stolen," February 26, 2019, `http://www.greenfieldreporter.com/2018/01/16/01162018dr_hancock_health_pays_ransom/`

[5]Zdnet, "Atlanta projected to spend at least $2.6 million on ransomware recovery," February 26, 2019, `https://www.zdnet.com/article/atlanta-spent-at-least-two-million-on-ransomware-attack-recovery`

[6]Denverpost, "Cyber attack on CDOT computers estimated to cost up to $1.5 million so far," February 26, 2019, `https://www.denverpost.com/2018/04/05/samsam-ransomware-cdot-cost/`

Most SamSam attacks are launched in the early morning or after midnight (of the target local time zone) when IT administrators are expected to be asleep or junior admin are on duty. Once installed on the victim machine, it begins searching for all backups on the local computer and all connected shares, looks for Windows Volume Shadow copies (the Windows built-in backup service), and deletes everything to prevent a victim from recovering their files. SamSam uses RSA-2048 encryption to encrypt victim files.

SamSam demands a high ransom to handle the decryption key. For example, the Hancock Health hospital paid 4 Bitcoins (equivalent to $55,000 at that time) to regain access to its data. The criminal group behind SamSam has generated about $6 million since their first attack.[7] SamSam ransoms are paid through Bitcoin. The waiting time for paying the ransom is seven days; after that, the ransom increases.

The criminals behind SamSam are continually developing it to evade detection. The ransom amount is also increasing dramatically, and the amount of acquired ransom in the past has helped the SamSam operators to invest more time and resources to employ more sophisticated techniques in its design, spread, attack, and deployment that has only been seen in espionage attacks. There is no sign of slowdown of SamSam ransomware attacks in the future, making it a severe threat, especially to U.S. organizations.

Note!   The criminals behind SamSam focus on attacking healthcare organizations, maybe because they think they are easier to attack and they are more willing to pay the ransom because of the sensitivity of patients records.

DMA Locker

This is another encryption ransomware that hit the Windows OS, first appearing at the beginning of 2016. The DMA Locker ransomware is known to spread mainly through the Remote Desktop Connection protocol in addition to other traditional methods. Once installed on the victim machine, it stops all applications used for backups and encrypts data using AES encryption without adding any extension to encrypted files. Instead, it adds a signature into the header of each infected file to recognize it. DMA Locker demands 2 Bitcoin (DMA version 2 and DMA version 3 requested 4 Bitcoin,

---

[7]Sophos, "SamSam: The (Almost) Six Million Dollar Ransomware," February 26, 2019, https://www.sophos.com/en-us/medialibrary/PDFs/technical-papers/SamSam-The-Almost-Six-Million-Dollar-Ransomware.pdf

while version 4.0 requested 1 BTC) as a ransom to handle the decryption key. The DMA Locker ransom note displays step-by-step instructions on how to pay the ransom. A distinguishing feature of this ransomware is its ability to decrypt victim files through the built-in feature available within the ransom note (see Figure 3-6).

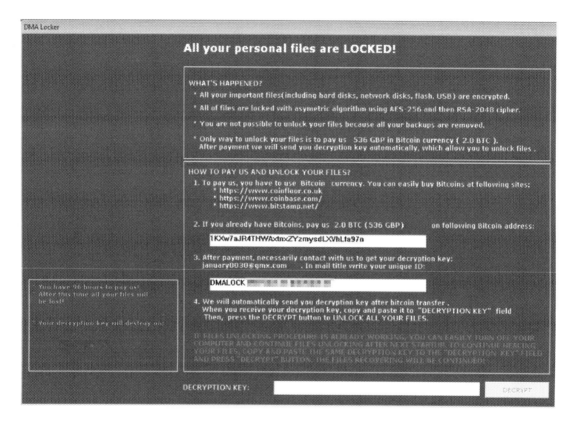

Figure 3-6. *DMA Locker version 2.0 ransom note showing step-by-step payment instructions*

WHAT IS A FILE SIGNATURE (HEADER)?

Most digital files have a signature located in the first 20 bytes of the file; this signature can be viewed by opening the subject file using Windows Notepad or any other text editor like Notepad++ (https://notepad-plus-plus.org). For example, we have an image file named diala.jpg; if we open the JPG file using a hex editor (I'm using HxD editor, which you can download from www.mh-nexus.de) and investigate its first 20 bytes, you should see the signature associated with the JPG file type (see Figure 3-7).

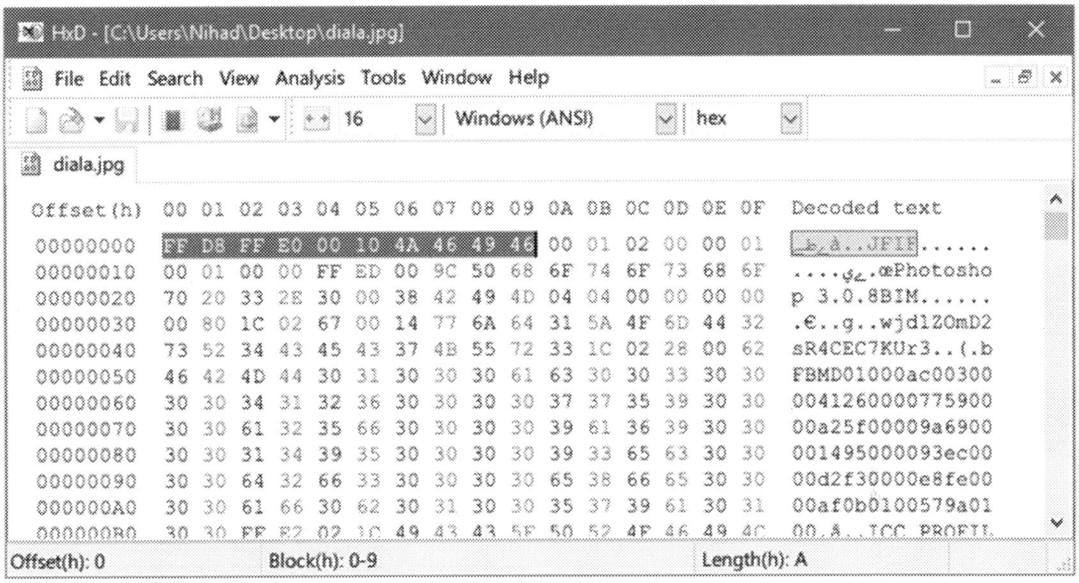

Figure 3-7. *Investigating file signature header*

In the same way, DMA Locker inserts its own signature into the infected files' header to distinguish it.

DMA Locker encrypts everything on the target machine except executables and Windows system files (it has a white list of folders and file extensions excluded from encryption) and adds autorun keys in the Windows registry for persistence through reboots. After the infection, the victim computer remains operational and can pay the ransom through it. DMA Locker has the ability to encrypt network shares and even unmapped network shares. The first version of DMA Locker generates one encryption key for all the files it encrypts on the victim machine; however, the new releases (beginning from version 2) of this ransomware create a new random AES key for each infected file and then encrypt the randomly generated key using the RSA algorithm.

CryptXXX

Another encryption ransomware targeting the Windows OS first appeared in April 2016; it was dropped by the Bedep Trojan horse, which in turn spread through the Angler exploit kit (EK). This ransomware family not only encrypts victim files; it also executes another information-stealing malware (the StillerX DLL module, which also can be deployed as a stand-alone tool) to steal Bitcoins and other information (e.g., e-mail clients' passwords, web browser passwords, VPN credentials, and cookies) from the victim computer and send them back to its operators through its C&C server. Some security researchers conclude that the group behind CrypXXX is the same group that was driving the Reveton ransomware because of the many similarities between them. The first version of CryptXXX encrypted victim files using the RSA-4096 algorithm and added the .crypt extension to the filename, while newer versions adopt different behaviors regarding naming victim files. For instance, some variations do not append any extension to encrypted files, while others append different extensions (e.g., .cryp1, .crypz, or a random string) and rename the entire file to something new. CryptXXX also has anti-sandboxing and anti-analysis capabilities and requests a relatively high ransom ($500) via Bitcoin. It leaves three types of readme files (de_crypt_readme.bmp, de_crypt_readme.txt, de_crypt_readme.html) on the victim machine to alert the owner about the infection and give instructions on how to pay the ransom (see Figure 3-8).

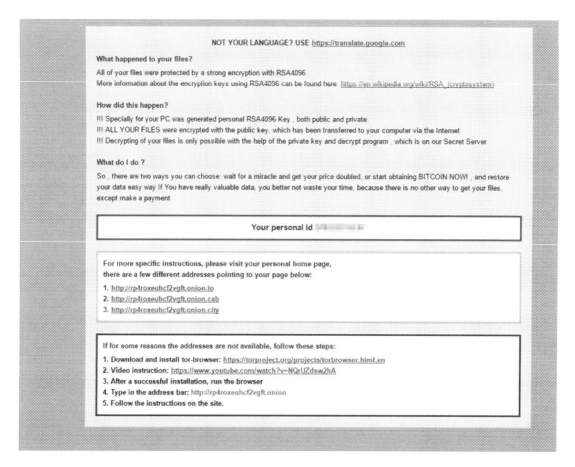

Figure 3-8. CryptXXX ransom payment instruction note (readme file)

CryptXXX version 2.0 denies access to the victim machine by locking the screen with the ransom alert.

A variation of CryptXXX named UltraCrypter is reported to have major errors with its payment system design, as this system was not able to provide the decryptor for victims after paying the ransom.[8]

In version CryptXXX 3.100, the developers behind CryptXXX shifted its distribution to the Neutrino exploit kit. This version has been updated to include more capabilities such as a network scanning capability to search and encrypt shared resources on the Windows domain and Windows Active Directory networks. The payment portal was also updated and connects directly to a web site hosted on the TOR network.

CryptoWall

CryptoWall is the successor to the obsolete CryptoLocker ransomware. CryptoWall is encryption ransomware that targets Windows-based machines; it spreads through malicious spam e-mails, exploit kits such as Nuclear and Angler, and malvertising campaigns. It is believed that CryptoWall was developed by the same criminal groups behind Cryptolocker, CryptoDefense, BitCrypt, and Cryptorbit. Once executed on the victim machine, CryptoWall writes its own registry autorun keys in the Windows registry to maintain its persistence through reboots. It then searches for all system restore points and Volume Shadow Copy files and destroys them to prevent the victim from restoring any file. Then it begins encrypting files using the RSA-2048 encryption algorithm. Ransom note files are named differently for each variant and are dropped on the infected system using different file formats such as HTML, TXT, URL, and PNG. These files will open automatically on the victim machine after successful infection. For example, CryptoWall 1.0 drops the following files onto the victim machine: `DECRYPT_INSTRUCTION.HTML`, `DECRYPT_INSTRUCTION.TXT`, and `DECRYPT_INSTRUCTION.URL`. Version 4.0 of CryptoWall drops the following files: `NSTRUCTIONS_47987A1B78.html`, `INSTRUCTIONS_47987A1B78.png`, and `INSTRUCTIONS_47987A1B78.txt` (The numbers in each file name are unique for each infected machine.) CryptoWall uses the TOR channel to communicate with its command-and-control server hosted on the TOR network. (One variant used the I2P anonymous network instead of TOR; however, it was discarded after a short time.)

---

[8]Bleepingcomputer, "UltraCrypter not providing Decryption Keys after payment. Launches Help Desk," February 26, 2019, https://www.bleepingcomputer.com/news/security/ultracrypter-not-providing-decryption-keys-after-payment-launches-help-desk/

WHAT IS THE I2P ANONYMOUS NETWORK?

I2P is an alternative anonymity network to TOR, and it supports common Internet activities such as web browsing, e-mail web site hosting, file sharing, and real-time chat.

Unlike TOR, whose focus is to access web sites from the normal Internet in addition to hosting anonymous web sites known as TOR services (has the `.Onion` domain extension), I2P is more directed toward accessing a closed, anonymous Internet, also known as a *darknet*, separate from the normal Internet. I2P protects communications from dragnet surveillance and monitoring by different third parties (governments, ISPs, etc.). Anyone running I2P can run an anonymous server through a so-called *eepsite*, which is accessible only within I2P networks using the `.i2p` top-level domain.

You can get I2P and learn more about it from its official web site (`https://geti2p.net/en/`).

CryptoWall has evolved over time and now has six major variants. The first variant appeared in November 2013 and was a complete clone of the CryptoLocker ransomware in terms of text and graphical user interface. The second variant came in February 2014 and was named CryptoDefense. However, a bug in its cryptography implementation that made it possible to restore victim files forced its operators to halt this variant.

In March 2014, CryptoWall developers released its first "official" version that carries its current name. CryptoWall 1.0 (see Figure 3-9) is a modern version of CryptoDefense that fixes its previous errors, making it more robust to attack systems. However, a flaw in its deletion function makes it possible to recover deleted victim backup files by using recovery software and other digital forensics techniques, as the ransomware was not overwriting the deleted backup files. Instead, it deleted them using the Windows API DeleteFile function, and data deleted using such technique can be recovered later if the victim machine has enough disk space at the time of infection. See Figure 3-10 for the CryptoWall 1.0 communication model.

What happened to your files?

All of your files were protected by a strong encryption with RSA-2048 using CryptoWall.

More information about the encryption keys using RSA-2048 can be found here: http://en.wikipedia.org/wiki/RSA_(cryptosystem)

What does this mean?

This means that the structure and data within your files have been irrevocably changed, you will not be able to work with them, read them or see them, it is the same thing as losing them forever, but with our help, you can restore them.

How did this happen?

Especially for you, on our server was generated the secret key pair RSA-2048 - public and private.

All your files were encrypted with the public key, which has been transferred to your computer via the Internet.

Decrypting of your files is only possible with the help of the private key and decrypt program, which is on our secret server.

What do I do?

Alas, if you do not take the necessary measures for the specified time then the conditions for obtaining the private key will be changed.

If you really value your data, then we suggest you do not waste valuable time searching for other solutions because they do not exist.

For more specific instructions, please visit your personal home page, there are a few different addresses pointing to your page below:

1.https://kpai7▓▓ ▓▓▓▓.torminater.com▓▓
2.https://kpai7▓▓ ▓▓▓▓.torchek.com/g▓
3.https://kpai7▓▓ ▓▓▓▓.way2tor.com/g▓

If for some reasons the addresses are not available, follow these steps:

1. Download and install tor-browser: http://www.torproject.org/projects/torbrowser.html.en
2. After a successful installation, run the browser and wait for initialization.
3. Type in the address bar: kpai7ycr7jxqkilp.onion/gctz
4. Follow the instructions on the site.

IMPORTANT INFORMATION:

Your Personal PAGE: https://kpai7ycr7jx▓▓▓▓ ▓▓▓ ▓▓▓ ▓▓▓▓▓
Your Personal PAGE(using TOR): kpai7yc▓ ▓▓▓▓ ▓▓▓▓▓
Your personal code (if you open the site (or TOR 's) directly): g▓▓

Figure 3-9. *Ransom note of CryptoWall version 1.0*

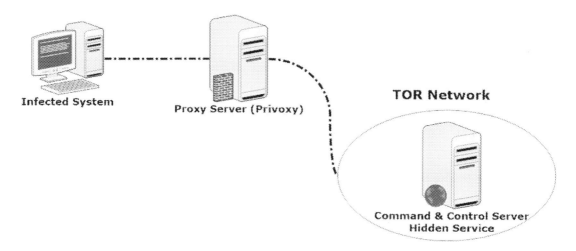

Figure 3-10. *Communication model of CryptoWall 1.0*

In each new version, CryptoWall operators tried to overcome the shortcomings in the previous version and add new functionalities. For example, CryptoWall version 2.0 uses a direct connection to the TOR network—where its C&C server is located—without passing the traffic via a proxy server. CryptoWall 3.0 uses a C&C hosted in the I2P anonymous network instead of TOR as the connection channel between the victim machine, and the C&C connection was direct without using any proxy server.

CryptoWall 4.0 returned to using the same communication model of version 1.0 with a small modification, as it inserts an additional proxy layer (a PHP script hosted on a compromised web site) between the victim machine and the Privoxy server.

Summary

In this chapter, I shed the light on the most common ransomware families according to their discovery date and gave some brief technical information about each family. Of course, there are scores of other ransomware families, but in this chapter, I focused on the most notable ones. To discover more ransomware families, please check out Table 3-1, which lists ransomware families according to the received Bitcoin payments. These statistics were taken from a study titled "Ransomware in the Bitcoin Ecosystem"[9] and cover the period from 2013 to mid-2017.

---

[9]Econinfosec, "Ransomware Payments in the Bitcoin Ecosystem," February 26, 2019, `https://weis2018.econinfosec.org/wp-content/uploads/sites/5/2018/05/WEIS_2018_paper_21.pdf`

Table 3-1. *Received Payment per Ransomware Family (2013–2017)*[10]

Family	Addresses	BTC	USD
Locky	6,827	15,399.01	7,834,737
CryptXXX	1,304	3,339.68	1,878,696
DMALockerv3	147	1,505.78	1,500,630
SamSam	41	632.01	599,687
Cryptolocker	944	1,511.71	519,991
GlobeImposter	1	96.94	116,014
WannaCry	6	55.34	102,703
CryptoTorLocker2015	94	246.32	67,221
APT	2	36.07	31,971
NoobCrypt	17	54.34	25,080
Globe	49	33.03	24,319
Globev3	18	14.34	16,008
EDA2	23	7.1	15,111
NotPetya	1	4.39	11,458

As you can see, different ransomware families use the same infection vectors to spread. Currently, malicious e-mail and exploit kits are the main methods used by ransomware operators to spread. Also note that most ransomware families use the Bitcoin cryptocurrency system to receive ransom payments and host their command-and-control server on the TOR darknet. The main differences between the ransomware families are the encryption algorithm used to encrypt victim files and the amount of ransom payment.

As malware authors continue their endeavor to write advanced malicious code and work to develop new spreading methods, you can expect to see future ransomware families with more capabilities to evade detection, automatically propagate to other

[10]Gosecure ,"Upcoming WEIS presentation: Ransomware Payment in the Bitcoin Ecosystem," February 26, 2019, https://gosecure.net/2018/06/18/ransomware-payment-in-the-bitcoin-ecosystem/

networks, and even infect IoT devices such as smart watches, smart TVs, and medical devices. Until then, the knowledge acquired from understanding the behaviors—in terms of the infection vector, communications models, and how they spread—of currently deployed ransomware families will help you to understand and defend against the new ransomware families that are going to appear in the future.

Now that you know about ransomware history, its main families, and how it infects and infiltrate systems, the big question is, what can enterprises and individuals do to protect against this emerging threat? Improved cybersecurity training and multiple layers of security defense are clearly part of the answer, and this what I cover in the second part of this book.

PART II

Ransomware Mitigation Strategies

CHAPTER 4

Endpoint Defense Strategies

How to Protect Endpoints from Ransomware Attacks

Ransomware attacks can hit almost any type of computing device, but endpoint devices still receive the largest number of ransomware incidents. Since the early days of the Internet, securing endpoint computers has always been considered the first line of defense against malware attacks (aside from firewalls and antivirus software).

Endpoint security is a term used to describe all technologies used to protect endpoint devices (or end-user devices) from cyberattacks. Securing endpoint devices is a key to protecting an entire enterprise's network from malicious attacks, as a compromised endpoint provides entry points for malicious actors to do their evil work.

Securing endpoints is not limited to installing antivirus solutions as some people may think. Several tasks are considered important elements in forming an endpoint defense strategy, such as configuring and hardening operating systems, updating and patching OSs and installed applications regularly, setting up usage policies that control which applications/scripts are allowed to run, deploying a data loss prevention (DLP) solution, implementing a data classification policy, using file and full-disk encryption, and using sandboxing technology. Optimizing your endpoint defense will help you to reduce the cyberattack surface as much as possible in addition to protecting your network and data from targeted and persistent attacks.

In this chapter, I teach you how to optimize your computing device to become more resistant to ransomware attacks. I also cover different methods to lower the attack surface of cyberattacks against endpoint devices, focusing primarily on ransomware threats. Please note there are many commercial endpoint security solutions on the market, and such solutions come bundled with rich security tools such as anti-malware,

© Nihad A. Hassan 2019
N. A. Hassan, *Ransomware Revealed*, https://doi.org/10.1007/978-1-4842-4255-1_4

firewalls, e-mail protection, antispam, web advisors, application control, device control, remote management, and the ability to sandbox applications for complete security. I will not recommend any specific product, as you can consider the security protection elements and countermeasures mentioned in this book as a features checklist for any product you aim to have.

Cybersecurity awareness training is an important element in any endpoint defense strategy; learn more about it in Chapter 6.

Note!   Endpoint devices are any Internet-capable computing device such as desktop computers, laptops, smartphones, tablets, Internet of Things (IoT) devices, printers, or other specialized hardware such as point-of-sale (PoS) terminals and smart meters.

Install Security Solutions

Antivirus software is still considered the first line of defense against ransomware attacks on endpoint devices. The term *antivirus* (AV) refers to the computer program responsible for detecting and removing malware infections.

There are many free antivirus solutions; nevertheless, they lack the necessary features to prevent advanced malware attacks such as ransomware. The main antivirus suites come bundled with a built-in firewall and other security protections such as antispam and antiphishing, which adds an extra layer of defense to prevent malware infections.

Note!   It is not advisable to install two antivirus products on one machine; this may lead to incompatibility issues. In a corporate environment, it is usual to see more than one AV solution, with one type installed on server gateways and another type on endpoint devices.

To select the best antivirus solution to protect against ransomware, you should first understand the different detection techniques employed by antivirus products to detect and block malware.

Antivirus Detection Techniques

Currently, there are five main methods used by antivirus vendors to detect, block, and remove malicious software.

Signature-Based Detection

This is the oldest approach used in antivirus products to detect malware. With this approach, the antivirus vendor discovers the malware first and then creates a unique signature for this type of malware. (The *signature* is a unique string of bits similar to a fingerprint that distinguishes a specific file's characteristics.) After that, the signature is tested to make sure it can be used successfully to capture this type of malware. Finally, the antivirus vendor pushes the new signature to its customers to update their client antivirus definition list. This detection technique is still widely used for traditional home antivirus solutions. However, it cannot fully detect advanced malware types that use polymorphic or encrypted code techniques to evade detection.

Behavior Analytics

In behavior detection, the antivirus program tries to identify the malware by looking at its behaviors such as if it is modifying the system by unpacking malicious code, deleting files, changing operating system "host" file content, monitoring keystrokes, or trying to connect with a remote server online. Such indicators can fire an alarm or block the attack before it continues.

Note!   An operating system *host file* is a system text file that exists on all major OSs and is used to map domain names to their associated IP addresses. Although it was replaced with the Domain Name System (DNS) a long time ago, it is still available in modern OSs as an alternative method for domain name resolution. In Windows, it can be found at `%SYSTEMDRIVE%\Windows\System32\drivers\etc\hosts`. Some malware types modify the OS host file to redirect the unaware user to a spoofed web site instead of the legitimate one.

Heuristics-Based Detection

In this detection type, the antivirus program uses different rules and algorithms to analyze its source code to discover any malicious intent. The examination of code structure can be done by running a simulated process of the suspected malware to see how it behaves if executed. Based on the test, the antivirus solution can classify the source code as a malicious or a legitimate program.

The major disadvantage of heuristics detection is the number of false positive alerts; it usually classifies many legitimate files as suspicious.

Cloud-Based Detection

As its name implies, in cloud-based detection, the suspicious file is sent to the antivirus vendor cloud infrastructure to analyze it instead of doing this locally. Cloud-based detection reduces the processing overhead on the end-user machine and shifts it to the cloud engine; however, the locally installed antivirus client still needs to use one or more of the previous detection techniques (signature, behavior, and heuristics) to capture suspicious files before sending them to the cloud for analysis. The main advantage of cloud-based detection is its ability to discover new threats more quickly as it can benefit from other users' scan results; in addition, it is less expensive than purchasing a full antivirus suite. The main disadvantage is its reliance on Internet connectivity to perform its duties.

Sandboxing

In sandbox detection, the antivirus program will run the suspicious file in a virtual environment where no harm can be done to the host machine when checking its behaviors and classifying it accordingly.

Which One Is the Best for Me?

Most antivirus vendors use more than one detection method to scan for malware. For instance, reliable endpoint antivirus products that use cloud-based detection use a mix of signature-based, behavior, and heuristic methods to identify suspicious files. On the other hand, modern antivirus products rely heavily on heuristics and behavioral analysis to protect computers from malware. The sandbox detection method needs time to identify suspicious files, so it is usually used on server machines.

Before buying an antivirus product, make sure it offers the following major features:

- Anti-malware, antispam, and antiphishing capabilities

- A USB scanner to scan USB devices for malware threats

- Regular updates installed automatically

- Integration with major e-mail client programs such as Microsoft Outlook and Mozilla Thunderbird to scan incoming/outgoing e-mail traffic and filtering spam e-mails

- Bundled with a personal firewall

- Tamper protection so malware cannot stop it without user knowledge

- A DNS protection feature

In addition to all these features, your chosen antivirus product should come from a major, reputable company. Big antivirus vendors have more resources to discover zero-day attacks than the smaller vendors.

Warning!   Antivirus protection alone is ineffective against ransomware attacks. Having an antivirus program is not a 100 percent effective solution to stopping ransomware. Previous attacks have shown that even with the deployment of more than one antivirus solution, corporations can still be infected by ransomware.

Note!   Why can't traditional antivirus solutions detect ransomware effectively? Phishing e-mail is the main attack vehicle of ransomware. This attack uses social engineering tactics to convince unsuspecting users to download and open malicious attachments to infect their machine with ransomware. In fact, humans are the weakest link, and ransomware depends heavily on human errors to infect and spread. This cannot be stopped without proper cybersecurity awareness training so that users can become aware of the latest cyberthreats and the infection methods.

Update OS and Installed Applications

Keep your OS and applications up-to-date and do not use discontinued software products. Your OS must be configured to update itself automatically; in addition, installed web browsers, along with their installed add-ons, and antivirus programs should both update automatically.

Using an unsupported OS is highly risky; for instance, Microsoft will no longer provide security updates or technical support for Windows XP and Vista. Windows 7 will follow them on January 14, 2020. Unsupported OSs can contain security holes that will not be patched by its manufacturer and consequently can be exploited by hackers to bypass antivirus and firewall defense to infect the target machine and consequently the connected network with malware.

Even if you are using a supported OS that receives updates, you are at risk if your update is broken and security updates are not installing correctly for some reason (e.g., a pirated OS will not install regular updates properly).

To configure Windows (applicable to Windows 7 and 8) to install updates automatically, go to Control Panel and select System. On the bottom left, click Windows Update. On the left side, click "Change settings," and from the drop-down menu, select "Install updates automatically (recommended)" (see Figure 4-1).

Figure 4-1. *Configuring Windows 8 to install updates automatically (applicable to Windows 7 also)*

In Windows 10, automatic updates are enabled by default.

As you saw in Chapter 2, an exploit kit is a popular method used by cybercriminals to infect a system with ransomware. After directing the unsuspecting user to the web site housing the exploit kit, the ransomware will execute and use a vulnerable application, such as Adobe Flash, the Java Runtime Environment (JRE), or Microsoft Silverlight, or an unpatched OS to run malware on the victim machine. To prevent an exploit kit from exploiting vulnerable applications, you should make sure that all installed applications are current.

This can be achieved automatically by using a software updater program that keeps all your installed programs (and other third-party tools) updated to the latest version. The following are some free software updaters to aid you in this task:

- Patch My PC (`https://patchmypc.com/homeupdaterdownload`)

- OUTDATEfighter (`https://www.spamfighter.com/OUTDATEfighter/Download_Download.asp`)

- Software Updater (`https://www.softwareupdater.com/download.php`)

Finally, you should not forget to update your device firmware, especially the networking devices such as routers and switches.

Virtualization Technology

Using virtualization technology allows a user to protect their machine from ransomware and other malware threats. By using a virtual machine, a user can execute programs, open e-mail attachments, download and install Internet programs, and visit compromised web sites safely without being afraid of infecting their operating system with malware, as the virtual machine will run in a sandbox isolated entirely from its host machine's operating system. Popular virtual machines include VirtualBox (`https://www.virtualbox.org`) and VMware Workstation Player (`www.vmware.com/products/player/playerproevaluation.html`).

Note!   An alternative method to running a complete OS on a virtual machine is to freeze your OS, making it unsusceptible to any changes. Toolwiz Time Freeze (`http://www.toolwiz.com/lead/toolwiz_time_freeze`) is a simple tool for making instant system restores. By turning on Time Freeze mode, the entire system will run inside a sandbox. Any change made to the system or to a user's stored files will be discarded upon reboot; only the files in the exclusion list will retain their updates (see Figure 4-2).

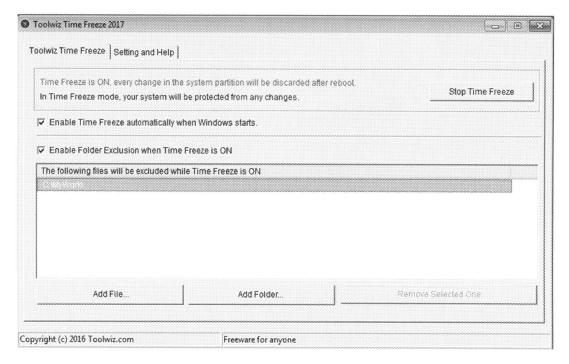

Figure 4-2. *Toolwiz Time Freeze activated with one folder in the exclusion list*

Secure Web Browsing

Web browsers are your window to the Web. Internet users use web browsers to socialize, make online purchases, download software, or send e-mails. Obviously, this makes web browsers a preferred target used by cybercriminals to attack their victims.

Note!   The main attack vectors of ransomware are e-mails, exploit kits, programs downloaded from the Internet, and social networking web sites. All these resources are usually accessed using web browsers.

Like with virtual machines, you can use the sandboxing technology to separate programs such as Internet browsers, e-mail clients, and other IM programs from the underlying operating system by running such programs inside sandbox software. In this way, you can assure that unwanted changes will not happen to your personal data and installed OS and programs, and you can also surf suspicious web sites safely, including ones prohibited by the installed antivirus solution, without being afraid of any type of malware infection. E-mail clients can also run inside the sandbox, allowing a user to open untrusted e-mail attachments without any fear of being infected with malware. In addition, running programs inside a sandbox application will consume fewer computing resources (processing and memory) compared with running a full OS inside a virtual machine. There are many sandbox programs. Shade Sandbox (`https://www.shadesandbox.com`) is a free reliable sandbox app for the Windows OS (see Figure 4-3).

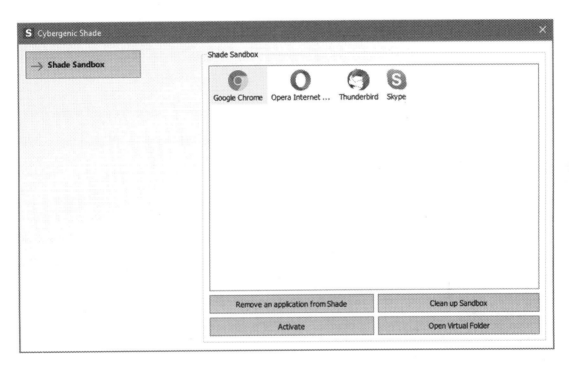

Figure 4-3. *Using the Shade Sandbox app to run locally virtualized applications*

Note!   Advanced ransomware families can detect a virtual environment to avoid detection and analysis. Although detecting a virtual environment is considered an advanced feature of some ransomware strains, this feature can be used against ransomware operators to stop their invasion. For example, a proof-of-concept experiment conducted by McAfee found that emulating a virtual environment on

79

the ordinary (physical) machine can protect it from some types of ransomware attack (e.g., the Locky ransomware family). The experiment found that the malware did not run, and the emulated machine was not infected.[1]

If you want to isolate your browsing activities from the underlying host OS without installing any software on your machine, then you can choose WEBGAP. WEBGAP is an online service that uses the browser isolation cybersecurity model to physically isolate an Internet user's web browser and their browsing activity away from the local machine and network (see Figure 4-4).

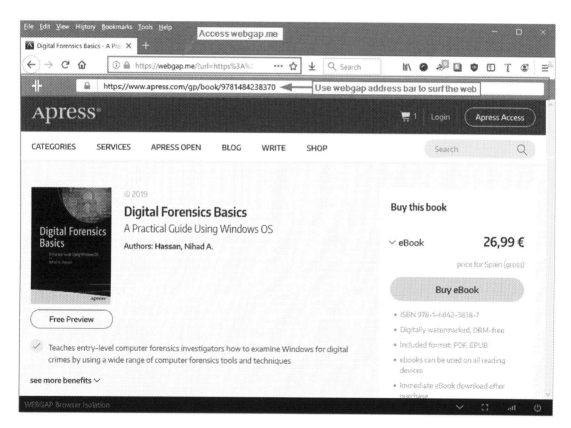

Figure 4-4. *Using the WEBGAP browser isolation service to surf the Web securely*

[1]Mcafee, "Stopping Malware With a Fake Virtual Machine" April 20, 2019.
https://securingtomorrow.mcafee.com/other-blogs/mcafee-labs/
stopping-malware-fake-virtual-machine

Block Web Page Redirect

Stopping web page redirects in a web browser will keep you safe from rogue sites and malicious links. All major web browsers can be configured to prevent redirects from happening. In this section, I demonstrate how to configure Firefox to prevent web page redirects.

Firefox has built-in phishing and malware protection; this feature works by checking the visited web sites and downloaded programs/files against a list of malicious links compiled from phishing web sites and other sites known to house malware. Firefox lists are updated every 30 minutes when enabling this feature; if a user tries to download something from a web site listed as malicious, Firefox will block the download immediately. To enable this feature, do the following:

1. Open Firefox, click the menu button in the top-right corner, and choose Options.

2. On the Firefox option page, click the Privacy & Security link in the left panel.

3. In the Permissions section, make sure the following settings are enabled: "Block popup windows" and "Warn you when websites try to install addons" (see Figure 4-5).

Figure 4-5. *Disabling pop-up windows under Firefox*

4. The next setting that you need to enable is "Block dangerous and deceptive content" (see Figure 4-6); you can find it in the Security section.

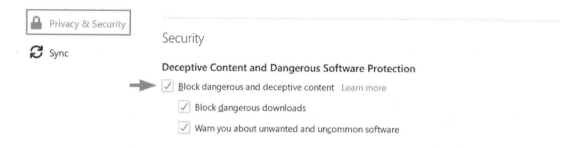

Figure 4-6. *Enabling phishing and malware protection under Firefox*

Finally, close Firefox and reopen it for the changes to take effect. To test this feature, go to the malware test site at `http://itisatrap.org/firefox/its-an-attack.html`. Firefox should block the site and display a warning message (see Figure 4-7).

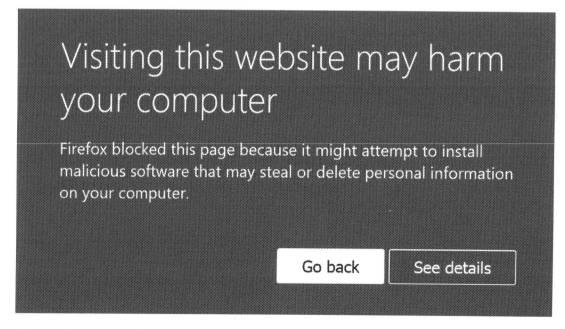

Figure 4-7. *Sample deceptive site warning when visiting a phishing site launched by Firefox*

Web Browser Add-ons

There are many web browser security add-ons that can help you increase your online privacy and can be beneficial in preventing ransomware attacks (e.g., blocking malicious advertisements and pop-ups that can redirect you to compromised web sites). For instance, I always encourage users to use open source software to assure maximum security when working online. Mozilla Firefox is still considered the only true open source browser of the main desktop browsers dominating the market today, so I will mention the security add-ons for this browser (although other versions of the same add-on are available for major web browsers such as Google Chrome and Opera).

- **Privacy Badger** (`https://www.eff.org/privacybadger`): Blocks spying ads and invisible trackers.

- **HTTPS Everywhere** (`https://www.eff.org/https-everywhere`): Encrypts communications with major web sites, making your browsing more secure.

- **NoScript** (`https://noscript.net`): Allows JavaScript, Java, Flash, and other plugins to be executed only by trusted web sites that are selected by the user. Configuring this add-on takes a little time as it stops all scripts by default, so the user needs to specify all the sites they trust; however, once it is up and running, it offers enhanced security against different online threats.

- **uBlock Origin** (`https://addons.mozilla.org/en-US/firefox/addon/ublock-origin`): General-purpose ad blocker (blocks ads, pop-ups, and trackers) with custom rules set by the user.

Warning!   Please note that some add-on providers may fool users and collect private data about browsing habits and even personal information without their consent, so it is advisable to check the developer's reputation before installing any browser extension and install it from `https://addons.mozilla.org` exclusively.

Defend Against Exploit Kits

Exploit kits need an entry point to start their malicious action. The entry point is usually a vulnerable application or unpatched OS. Making sure that your OS is current and all installed applications and other third-party plugins are updated to the latest version should protect you from the majority of attacks delivered via exploit kits. Of course, this doesn't apply to zero-day vulnerabilities, which are nearly impossible to stop.

Disable Macros in Office Files

Microsoft Office macros use the Visual Basic for Applications (VBA) programing language to perform some advanced and repetitive tasks in the Microsoft Office suite, especially in Excel and Word, to increase user productivity. This feature can be exploited to install ransomware on the unsuspecting user's machine. Macros are by default disabled in recent editions of Microsoft Office; make sure not to enable them in documents downloaded from the Internet or received via e-mail messages from untrusted sources.

The majority of ransomware is delivered via Microsoft Office in macros received through spam e-mails. To counter this risk, open any Office files sent via e-mails using Office viewer programs or using the Google Docs online viewer (`https://www.google.com/docs/about`) instead of running such files using the full Office suite.

Disable Windows Script Host

Windows Script Host (WSH) is a scripting language that comes associated with most Windows OS versions since 98. A WSH script usually has a `.vbs` extension and is written in VBScript by default, although other languages can be used such as JavaScript and Perl. WSH scripts can automate any normal task performed by Windows. This is useful, but it brings serious security issues when exploited by malicious actors to create scripts that execute/download ransomware or other malware payloads when less experienced users execute the script inadvertently (e.g., click malicious scripts sent via an e-mail attachment).

To counter the security risks associated with WSH, it is advisable to disable this feature on all endpoint devices and on servers when it is not used intensively by system administrators. To disable the WSH functionality for the current user, follow these steps:

1. Open the Windows Registry Editor by pressing the Windows+R keys and then type regedit.

2. Navigate to HKEY_CURRENT_USER\Software\Microsoft\Windows Script Host\Settings\.

3. Create a new REG_DWORD key by right-clicking the right pane, selecting New, selecting DWORD, naming it **Enabled**, and assigning a value of 0 to it (see Figure 4-8).

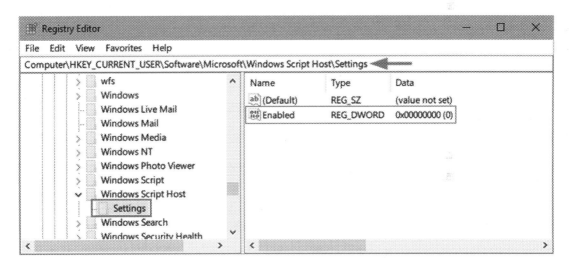

Figure 4-8. *Creating a new DWORD key to disable the WSH feature for the current user*

To make sure it works correctly, create a new text file, change its extension to .vbs, and try to run it. A pop-up message should appear saying that access is disabled (see Figure 4-9).

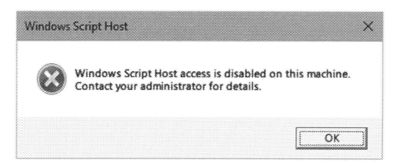

Figure 4-9. *A warning message when trying to execute a VBS script when the WSH feature is disabled*

To restore the WSH functionality, just delete the Enabled registry key (or change its value to 1).

Use a Least Privilege Account

Few ransomware strains need administrative privileges to operate properly, as most ransomware families rely on the privilege level of the currently logged-in user to do their malicious work. Nevertheless, using a low-privilege user account (Windows calls it the Standard account) is still considered an important countermeasure against different types of malware attacks. For instance, a limited user account cannot install programs or make important modifications to the OS (e.g., adding or modifying registry keys). Besides, some ransomware strains (e.g., Ryuk family) need admin privileges to execute and begin their work. As you already know, malware is a malicious computer program, meaning that the same restriction applies to it when infecting a user with limited privileges. Many studies show that using a limited account will help limit most malware infection.

Note!   94 percent of Microsoft vulnerabilities can be mitigated by using a standard limited user account.[2]

---

[2]Computerworld, "94% of Microsoft vulnerabilities can be easily mitigated" April 20, 2019. https://www.computerworld.com/article/3173246/94-of-microsoft-vulnerabilities-can-be-easily-mitigated.html

Tip!   When using your computer for Internet browsing, creating/editing Microsoft Office files, or opening e-mail attachments, it is always advisable to use a limited privilege Windows account (the Standard account). This tactic will stop different types of malware from infecting your machine and will prevent modern encryption ransomware from deleting Volume Shadow Copies (when the VSS service is enabled). Thus, you can restore the encrypted files from VSS Snapshot after a ransomware infection.

To set up a Standard user account on Windows 10, open Windows Settings and select Accounts. Then select "Family & other people" in the left pane and click "Add someone else to this PC" (see Figure 4-10).

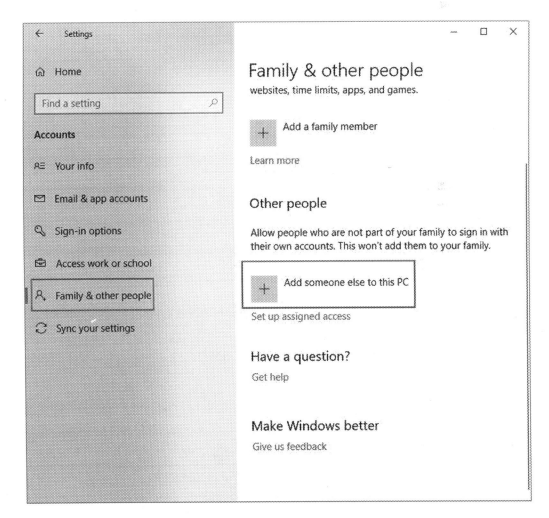

Figure 4-10.   *Creating a new user account on Windows 10 (version 1803)*

The new User Creation Wizard appears. Select "I don't have this person's sign-in information" and select "Add a user without a Microsoft account." Now enter a username and password and answer the three security questions needed to recover your account in case you forget the password. Click Next, and you are done.

To change the current Windows account type, go to Settings, select Accounts, and select "Family & other people" in the left pane. Now in the right pane, under "Other people," select the account you want to modify and click "Change account type." You have two options: Administrator and Standard (see Figure 4-11).

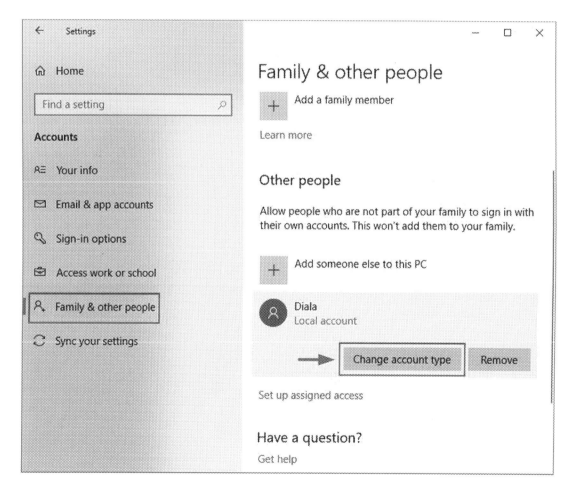

Figure 4-11. *Changing the account type on Windows 10*

Beginning with Windows Vista, Microsoft introduced User Account Control (UAC). This is a security feature that prevents unauthorized changes to the operating system without user consent. Such changes can be triggered by applications, users, ransomware (that needs administrative privilege), or other forms of malware. UAC prompts appear when trying to make any modification to OS files and displays the program name trying to make this change; if the active user has an administrator account, the UAC prompt will look similar to the one in Figure 4-12. If the user wants the changes to take effect, they need to click Yes.

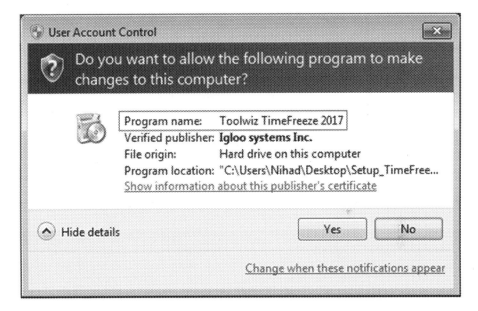

Figure 4-12. *UAC prompt in Windows 7 for a user with Administrator account privilege wanting to execute an installer*

To change the UAC under Windows 10, go to Control Panel and select Security and Maintenance on the left side. Select Change User Account Settings in the new window and move the slider up to "Always notify" (see Figure 4-13).

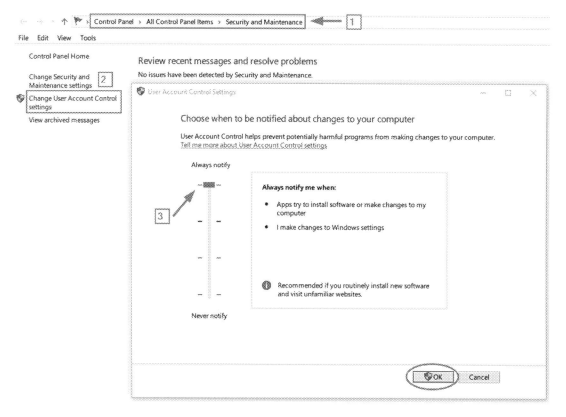

Figure 4-13. *Changing UAC settings under Windows 10 (also applicable to Windows 8.1 and 8)*

Although modern malware can bypass that UAC and infect the system without triggering a UAC prompt, enabling it, especially for users with admin privilege, can still prove beneficial in many instances.

Do Not Install Pirated Software

Many Internet users tend to install pirated software to save costs and download them from peer-to-peer file sharing networks (e.g., Torrent). Pirated programs usually come bundled with an executable program named Crack, Patch, or Keygen to unlock the pirated program trial version and make it work like the paid version. The pirated software might be disguised ransomware that will install silently upon executing it.

Note!   A study by F-Secure found that the WannaCry ransomware, which exploits a flaw in the Server Message Block (SMB) in Microsoft Windows, infected a large number of machines in China and Russia. This was because a large number of users in those two countries were using pirated copies of the Windows OS that could not receive regular updates. This makes the problem persist even after Microsoft has patched the vulnerability.[3]

USB Thumb Drive Security

Infecting computers with malware using USB thumb drives is an old infection method. Although it has somehow lost its novelty these days as users are now relying heavily on cloud services for transferring data, this attack vector is still actively used by malicious actors to spread malware. If the USB flash drive is infected with ransomware, the victim does not only risk damaging the files stored on the active machine; modern ransomware strains will automatically propagate to infect all connected devices on the same network.

Note!   The famous Stuxnet malware was delivered to the Iranian nuclear plant using an infected thumb drive.

It is strongly recommended that you avoid plugging untrusted USB devices into your work or home machine, especially ones found in public locations. If you want to see the contents of a suspicious USB thumb drive, make sure to open it on a disconnected machine with a limited-privilege account (the User account). Your antivirus program should scan USB devices automatically before mounting them; always consult an antivirus features list for such a capability before buying it.

---

[3]f-secure, "What You Need to Know About WannaCry Now" April 20, 2019. https://blog.f-secure.com/what-you-need-to-know-about-wannacry-now

Warning!   I recommend not plugging untrusted USB devices into your computer at all! Even if you have followed all the precautionary steps in this book, some advanced malware types come hard-coded inside the USB firmware, and this area cannot be accessed or scanned by antivirus solutions. Malicious USB drives can bring permanent damage to your hardware. For instance, USB Killer is a USB stick that sends 220 volts once plugged into a victim machine, frying its hardware and making it useless.[4]

Avoid Public Phone Chargers

In a juice jacking cyberattack, a malicious actor can gain access to your mobile computing device (smartphone, tablet, or laptop) when using the public charging outlets that exist in many public places. The risk is not limited to gaining unauthorized access to your device, as the malicious actor can inject malware (e.g., ransomware) into your device that can spread later to other devices when you connect your device to your home or corporate network.

Having a portable power bank with you to charge your mobile device when necessary is a countermeasure for this threat.

Change Important File Extensions

This trick can be effective to prevent damage caused by many types of ransomware strains; for example, the WannaCry ransomware searches and encrypts specific file extensions such as Microsoft Office files (e.g., `.doc`, `.docx`, `.xls`, `.xslx`, `.ppt`, `.pptx`, `.etc`), different backup archive file types (e.g., `.zip`, `.rar`, `.bakcup`, `.bak`), and popular image/video file formats. By changing your important files' extensions to something arbitrary, you can avoid many types of ransomware. For example, if your backup is stored as `myfiles.backup`, change the extension to anything else (e.g., for example, your last name!).

---

[4]Dailymail, "The gadget killer: USB drive can instantly fry everything from your TV to your computer by sending 220 volts through them" April 20, 2019 `https://www.dailymail.co.uk/sciencetech/article-3272862/The-USB-drive-instantly-FRY-TV-computer-sending-220-volts-them.html`

Mobile Device Security

Mobile devices, especially ones running the Android system, are a primary target for ransomware attacks. The following security measures can help you to strengthen your mobile device's defense against ransomware attacks:

- Avoid rooting your device. This will give you admin access and expose your OS files to malicious modifications.

- Make sure your device OS and installed applications are current.

- Always install applications from a trusted source (e.g., Google Play for Android and Apple Store for Apple devices). Third-party app stores can be risky.

- Prevent installing apps from unknown sources.

- Grant Google access to scan your Android device for security risks.

- Like e-mails received on your desktop or laptop, make sure to avoid clicking suspicious links in e-mails or SMS messages.

- Install a dedicated mobile security solution for protecting your device from malware.

- When installing a new app, check what permissions it needs.

- In a corporate environment, make sure to set up a blacklist of disallowed apps.

- Back up your mobile device data to an external offline storage device continually.

Back Up Your Data

Malware, user errors, and computer crashes can put your valuable data at risk at any time. For instance, the only way to restore your data without paying a ransom after a ransomware attack is to have a backup copy of your infected data.

This chapter covers the endpoint side of countermeasures against ransomware attacks, so as a user you should consider having a good backup of all your important data as they are modified, and you should also consider disconnecting the backup storage media (external hard drive, thumb drive, magnetic tape) from the machine and from any other networked device once the backup is finished. Always check your backup files to make sure they are accessible on the backup device in case you need them suddenly. Finally, do not rely solely on cloud storage backup. For example, if you configure your machine to back up your important files to the cloud and a ransomware attack hit your machine, the backed-up data may get overwritten with the new version that is infected and encrypted by the ransomware.

In this section, I will list different backup solutions a user can implement to make sure their crucial data always remains secure.

Windows Backup Function

Windows has a dedicated built-in utility to back up your data onto external media. To access the backup utility in Windows 10, press Windows+I, select Update & Security, and select Backup. From here you have two options:

- Use the File History utility to back up your important folders, such as Desktop, Contacts, and Favorites, to a removable media or to a network location. You can also configure the File History utility to add/remove additional folders to the default backup routine by clicking "More options" (see Figure 4-14).

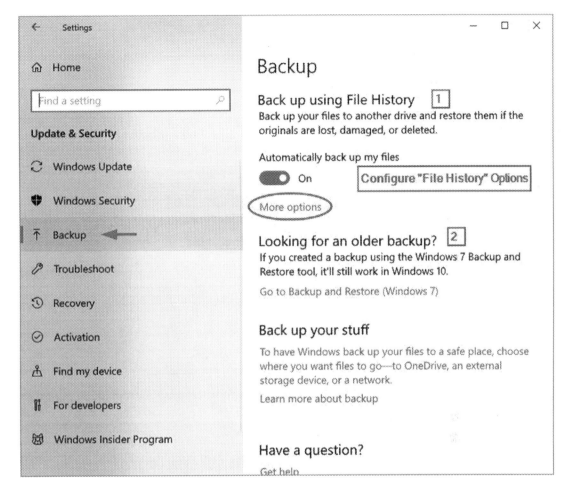

Figure 4-14. *Using and configuring the Windows 10 built-in backup*

- You can also use the old Backup and Restore (Windows 7) utility to create a full system image of your Windows drive (and all personal files stored within it) or to restore files from system image backups created in previous editions of Windows. Keep in mind that if you have a system image backup, you cannot restore individual files from it.

Third-Party Backup

If you prefer to use third-party backup software, here are two free options:

- **Comodo Backup** (`https://www.comodo.com/home/backuponlinestorage/backupfirsttimesetup.php`): Comodo is a free backup tool that is easy for casual computer users; using Comodo Backup, you can back up data to a local drive, to optical media like a CD/DVD/BD disc, to a network folder, to an external drive, or to an FTP server; or the data can be sent to a recipient over e-mail. The backup can be divided into pieces and protected with a password. Recovering data is easy and needs only a few clicks.

- **Cobian Backup** (`www.cobiansoft.com/cobianbackup.htm`): This is a free (even for commercial use) multithreaded program that can be used to back up your files, directories, or even complete drives to another location on the same local computer or to another one on your network. The FTP backup is also supported in both directions (download and upload). The resulting backup file can be divided into multiple pieces and protected with a password for additional security.

Enable the Shadow Copy Feature in Windows

Volume Shadow Copy (also known Volume Snapshot Service [VSS]) is a backup technology available in Windows beginning in Windows XP. The backup copies taken using VSS are called *snapshots* and can be created either automatically by the system or manually by the user. These snapshots can be stored on a local hard drive or on removable media storage. It is highly advisable to enable this feature on your Windows machine (especially on the volume containing your personal data). To do so, follow these steps (applicable to Windows 7/8/10):

1. Open Windows Control Panel.

2. Go to System.

3. On the left side, select System Protection.

4. The System Properties window appears; select the System Protection tab.

5. Select a drive and click Configure.

6. Select "Turn on system protection." In Windows 7, this option is called "Restore system settings and previous versions of files."

7. Click Apply and then the OK button (see Figure 4-15).

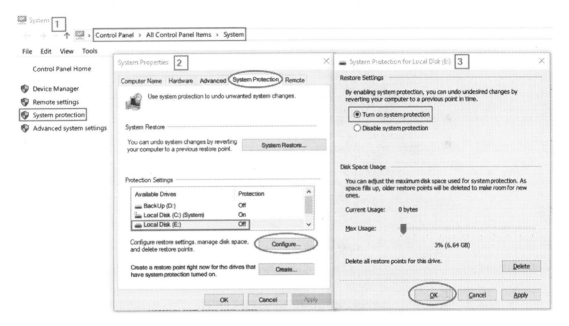

Figure 4-15. *Enabling the Volume Shadow Copy feature in Windows 7/8/10*

The VSS feature is a nice backup feature that enables Windows users to run a silent backup service while using their computer at full capacity. However, keep in mind that VSS is not meant to replace the regular data backup routine that should be configured to run frequently to back up your important data to an external safe location.

Tip!   To list available VSS snapshots on your machine or recover a specific file or folder from an old Windows restore point, you can use one of these two tools:

- ShadowCopyView (http://www.nirsoft.net/utils/shadow_copy_view.html) lists all restore points of your hard drive created by the Volume Shadow Copy service of Windows and allows you to extract files/folders from any snapshot (see Figure 4-16).

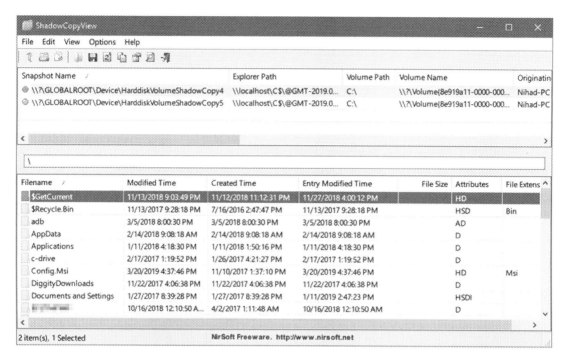

Figure 4-16. *Using ShadowCopyView to list/view existing restore points contents in Windows*

- ShadowExplorer (`www.shadowexplorer.com`) can browse old restore point contents (VSS snapshots) and extract individual files/folders from it.

Warning!   Modern encryption ransomware strains delete Volume Shadow Copies snapshots on the victim machine. Recovering deleted snapshots is not always possible and requires you to use sophisticated tools like the one used in digital forensic examination.

Configure Windows to Better Fight Ransomware

Hardening clients and servers is essential to limit the attack surface from both internal and external sources. The process of hardening a Windows client is different from a Windows server, because they are used in a completely different context. In this section, I give advice on hardening a stand-alone Windows machine. In the next chapter, I give essential tips for implementing security controls in a corporate environment context.

Show File Extensions

File extensions come hidden by default in Windows. Obviously, this makes recognizing potentially malicious files harder. For example, an executable ransomware file could have the extension `filename.docx.exe` and display a Microsoft Word icon; in this case, only the `.docx` extension would appear, making this file look harmless. To view the file extension on Windows 10, go to Control Panel and select File Explorer Options. In Windows 7, select Control Panel and Folder Options, go to the View tab, and deselect the option "Hide extensions for known file types" (see Figure 4-17).

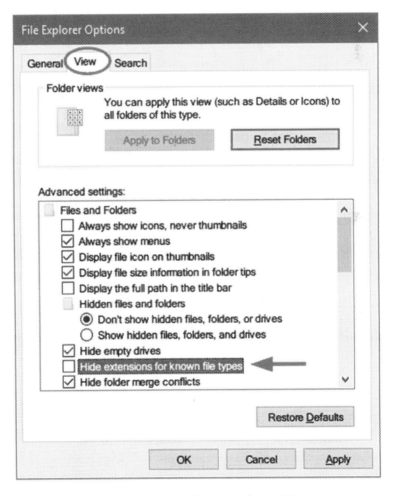

Figure 4-17. *Showing file extensions in the Windows OS*

Disable AutoPlay

Whenever you insert a removable storage device such as a USB thumb drive, external hard drive, CD/DVD/Blu-ray disk, or SD card into your machine, Windows will examine its contents and display the AutoPlay pop-up window asking you what action you want to perform with the inserted media.

The Windows AutoRun feature (the AutoPlay feature in Windows is part of AutoRun) is turned on by default on older Windows editions, allowing malicious programs to run from an external device as soon as they are inserted into a computer. Beginning from Windows Vista, Microsoft lowered this security risk by displaying the AutoPlay dialog whenever a removable media is inserted and asking the user what they want to do with it. Although modern Windows editions stop executing AutoRun automatically, the user is still one step away from running a potentially malicious program if they select to run a program in the AutoPlay dialog. For this reason, it is advisable to turn off both features to increase the protection against a USB malware attack.

To disable the AutoPlay feature in Windows (on Windows editions from 7 to 10), go to Control Panel, select AutoPlay, and uncheck the "Use AutoPlay for all media and devices" box; finally, click the Save button (see Figure 4-18).

Figure 4-18. *Disabling the Windows AutoPlay feature in Windows 10*

AutoRun is different from AutoPlay. While AutoPlay displays a pop-up window, AutoRun will search for the `autorun.inf` file, which automatically executes the associated program (could be a malware), specified in the `autorun.inf` file, each time the USB drive or disk is accessed. (This behavior is in old Windows versions, as mentioned.) This may result in infecting your computer with malware and, after that, spreading the infection to other devices residing on the same network. To mitigate this risk, it's highly recommended that you disable the AutoRun feature as well. In the following steps, we will show you how to disable both AutoPlay and AutoRun by using Windows Group Policy.

To disable AutoPlay using Windows Group Policy, do the following:

1. Access Group Policy Editor by typing **gpedit.msc** in the search box of the Windows Start menu.

2. Navigate to Computer Configuration ➤ Administrative Templates ➤ Windows Components ➤ AutoPlay Policies (see Figure 4-19).

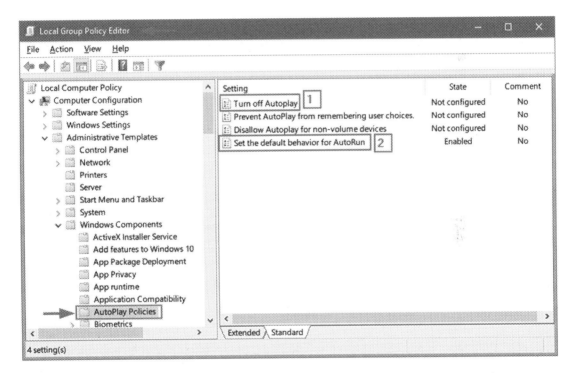

Figure 4-19. *Accessing AutoPlay Policies under Windows 10 using Local Group Policy Editor*

3. Double-click the Turn Off AutoPlay item in the right pane. In the pop-up, select the option Enabled, go to the Options section, and make sure "All drives" is selected (see Figure 4-20). Finally, click Apply and then OK.

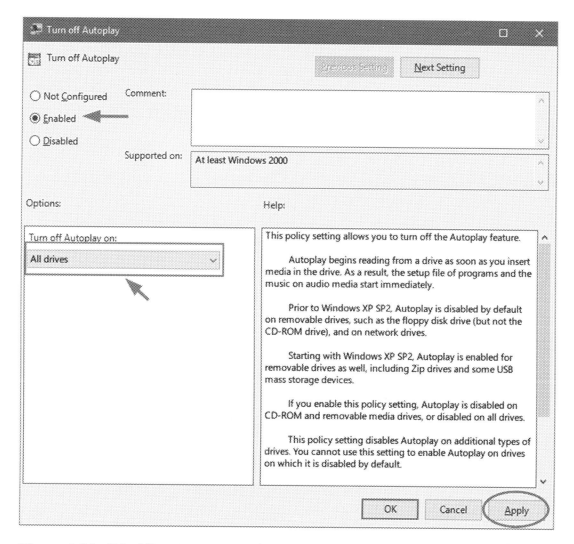

Figure 4-20. *Disabling AutoRun under Windows 10 using Local Group Policy*

Now, to disable the AutoRun feature, you need to set another item under AutoPlay Policies. Double-click "Set the default behavior for AutoRun" in the right pane; in the pop-up window, make sure it is enabled as in Figure 4-21. Finally, click Apply and then OK.

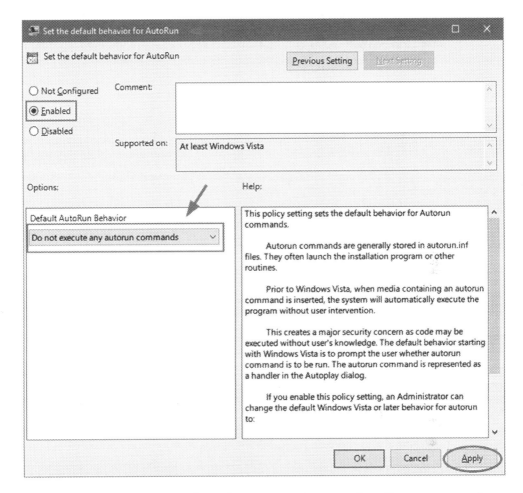

Figure 4-21. *Preventing Windows from executing any AutoRun commands*

Disable Remote Desktop Protocol

Remote Desktop Protocol (RDP) allows a user to remotely access their PC, but this protocol can be exploited to infect the machine with ransomware. To harden your RDP access, follow these steps:

- Use a strong password for your RDP access, with at least 16 alphamerical characters.

- Make sure that Network Level Authentication (NLA) is enabled for your RDP connection by going to Control Panel and selecting System. In the left panel, select "Advanced system settings" and go to the Remote tab (see Figure 4-22).

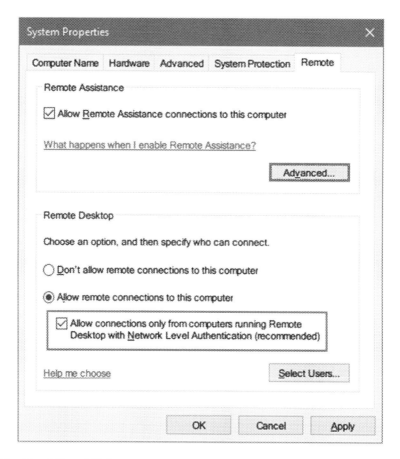

Figure 4-22. *Enabling NLA*

- Change the RDP default port number from 3389 to something else; this should add an extra layer of security to mislead port scanning tools. To change the RDP default port number, do the following:

    1) Open the registry editor by pressing Windows+R, type regedit, and press Enter.

    2) Now, navigate to HKEY_LOCAL_MACHINE\SYSTEM\ CurrentControlSet\Control\Terminal Server\ WinStations\RDP-TCP.

    3) Find the PortNumber item in the right pane and double-click to open it.

4) Change the base to show a decimal value, and change the
    number from 3389 to something else such as 4566.

5) Click OK to save your changes (see Figure 4-23), and reboot
    your machine for the change to take effect.

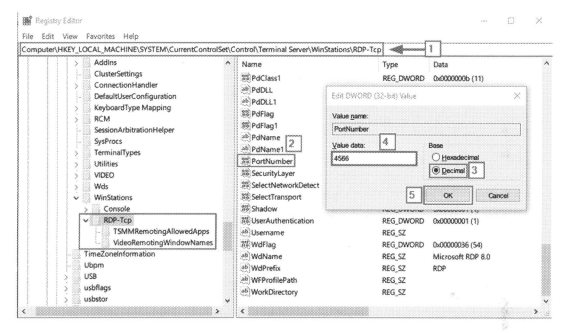

Figure 4-23. *Changing the RDP default port number*

- Use a reliable VPN service before initiating the RDP session. If you do
  not know how to select the best VPN service, I wrote a detailed guide
  about this issue at `https://www.secjuice.com/how-to-choose-a-`
  `virtual-private-network-vpn-provider/`.

- Make sure your OS is always patched and up-to-date to prevent any
  exploit to the RDP protocol that may result in compromising your
  system.

Finally, ask yourself this question: do you really need an RDP connection? If the
answer is no, then the most secure choice is to disable it.

Enable Software Restriction Policies

Regardless of whether the active user has a limited-privilege account, advanced malware can still infect their machine and propagate to other places across the network that the user can access. Malware can achieve this persistence on limited accounts by copying itself to the user's home directory to launch each time a user logs in to their machine. To counter such risks in both home and corporate environments, Microsoft has a simple and great security mechanism built into Windows to stop executing malicious code called *software restriction policies* (SRP).

In this section, I show you how to activate SRP using a stand-alone computer. If you are working in a corporate environment, the SRP group policy can be enabled on all corporate network endpoints using the Microsoft Active Directory domain service.

Warning!   SRP is not an antivirus program and does not mean to replace one. SRP cannot prevent malware from copying itself onto the subject machine's hard drive. However, it can prevent malware existing on the hard drive or on attached removable media drives from being executed.

SRP is a Group Policy feature available in all Windows editions except Windows Home versions. SRP allows administrators to create a restrictive environment on the Windows OS to control the execution of untrusted applications and scripts. For instance, by using SRP, you can control which applications/scripts can run from any directory within the system. For example, you can use SRP to tell Windows to execute programs from specific locations such as `C:\Windows`, `C:\Program Files`, and `C:\Program Files` (x86) while preventing this functionality everywhere else.

When ransomware hits a user logged in with a Standard account, it will usually copy itself into the user's home directory. A Standard Windows account does have permission to write to normal Windows directories (e.g., Windows, Program Files, and Program Files (x86)). In such a case, files downloaded from the Internet and e-mail attachments in addition to unzipped files are usually stored in the %APPDATA% folder under the current user home directory. By enabling the SRP policy, you can prevent ransomware and other malware types from executing from the home directory.

To enable SRP using Windows 10, follow these steps:

1. Go to the Windows Start menu and type **gpedit.msc** to launch the
    Windows Group Policy Editor.

2. Navigate to Computer Configuration ➤ Windows Settings ➤
    Security Settings ➤ Software Restriction Policies (see Figure 4-24).

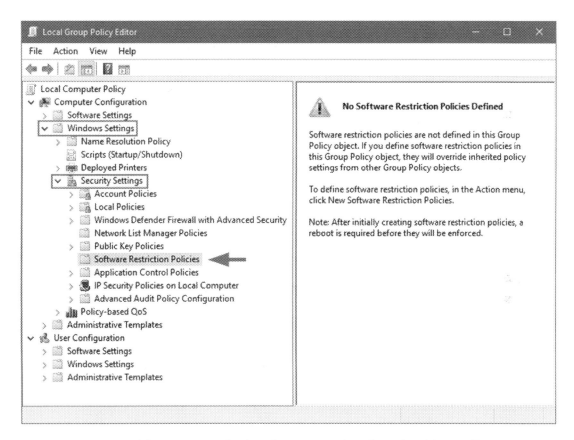

Figure 4-24. *Enabling SRP in the local Group Policy (applicable to all supported Windows versions)*

3. Right-click the Software Restriction Policies folder and select New
    Software Restriction Policies (see Figure 4-25).

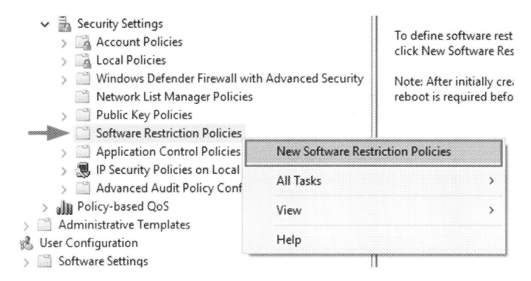

Figure 4-25. *Creating a new SRP policy*

4. In the right pane, double-click the Enforcement item to configure it, as shown in Figure 4-26.

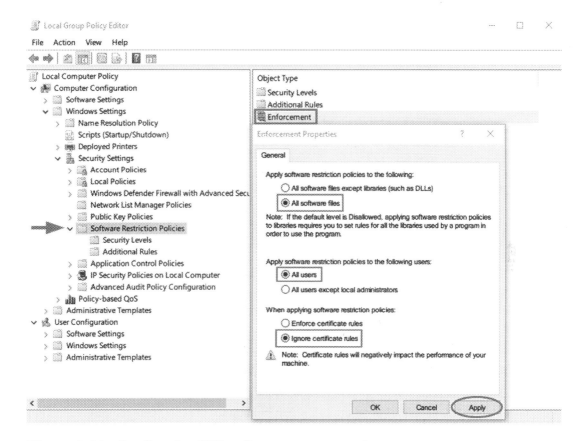

Figure 4-26. *Configuring SRP enforcement properties*

5. Now, you need to set the security level of your SRP policy; there
    are three options.

    •   **Disallowed**: The software will not run, regardless of the access
        rights of the user.

    •   **Basic User**: This allows the program to execute as a user who
        does not have Administrator access rights but can still access
        resources accessible by normal users.

    •   **Unrestricted**: The software access rights are determined by the
        access rights of the user.

In this case, you need to restrict the execution of applications and scripts, so
double-click Security Levels, right-click Disallowed, and select "Set as default" (see
Figure 4-27).

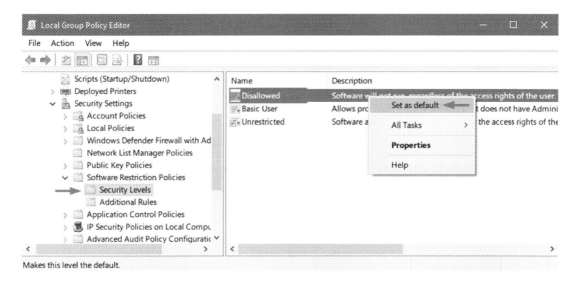

Figure 4-27. *Setting up a security level for the SRP policy*

6. To see the default paths where authorized software can run,
    double-click the Additional Rules folder; you will find two paths
    authorized (`C:\=Windows` and `C:\Program Files`). All programs
    stored within these two paths can run (see Figure 4-28). You
    can add additional paths/folders that will be able to launch
    applications. All you need to do is to right-click Additional Rules
    and select New Path Rule (see Figure 4-29). Now, in the New
    Rule Path configuration window, enter the path or click Browse
    to select one, and in the "Security level" drop-down menu, select
    Unrestricted (see Figure 4-30). To run programs from any of these
    additional paths, the subject program must load its libraries from
    the `C:\Windows\` and `C:\Program Files\` paths.

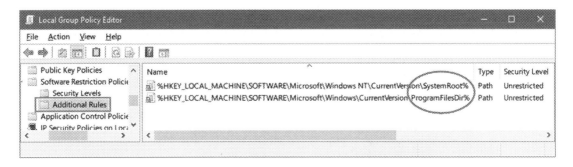

Figure 4-28. *Additional Rules folder listing default paths configured to allow programs to run*

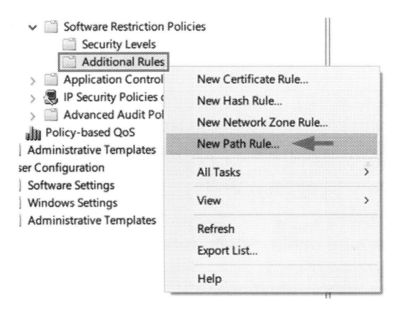

Figure 4-29. *Adding New Path Rule in the SRP policy to override the default security level*

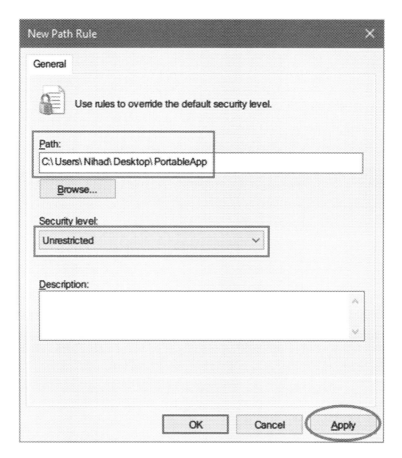

Figure 4-30. *Defining New Path Rule and specifying its security level; in this example, all programs stored within the specified path can run without restriction*

7. Finally, click Apply and then OK.

If a user tries to execute a program from a disallowed path, they will get the error message shown in Figure 4-31.

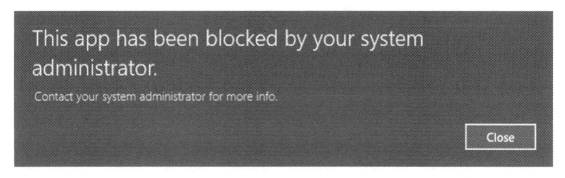

Figure 4-31. *Error message for a program executing from a disallowed path or having its libraries loaded from a disallowed path*

> **Note!**   Windows AppLocker is a new security feature for controlling software usage on Windows computers. First introduced in Windows 7, AppLocker replaces the Software Restriction Policies feature and is usually used in corporate environments. You'll learn more about it in the next chapter.

Summary

Endpoint defense should be the first line in a multilayer defense strategy. Most users understand the word *endpoint* as the last line of defense, but this is completely wrong. At endpoints, the user creates, processes, and stores their precious data, making it the preferred place for cybercriminals to begin their attack and to spread the infection to other places within the network. As the number of employees working remotely or using public WiFi access points to connect to their corporate network increases, protection of endpoint devices becomes an even higher priority for businesses.

In this chapter, I covered the general steps needed to protect endpoint devices from malware attacks, focusing on the ransomware threat. Endpoint security is not limited to installing anti-malware and other security software. For instance, enforcing software rules, using a limited privileged account, discovering vulnerabilities, and making sure your OS and required third-party applications are regularly patched and current will vastly reduce the opportunity for attackers to gain entry to your network through endpoints.

There are many commercial endpoint security vendors out there, many of which have developed products with advanced capabilities that surpass traditional antivirus solutions. Protecting your endpoint device with a commercial product is recommended for individual users (especially those with limited IT security experience) aiming to have advanced protection against today's growing sophisticated cyberattacks, while applying such solutions in organizations needs careful planning. Organizations also need to compare different products features to install the best one to fit their needs.

In the next chapter, we will continue our discussion of protective techniques to prevent a ransomware attack, but this time in an enterprise environment.

CHAPTER 5

Enterprise Defense Strategies Against Ransomware Attacks

Protection Against Ransomware Attacks on Corporate Environment

Governments and corporation networks are primary targets for cybercriminals; they contain valuable proprietary information such as trade secrets and financial information or hold sensitive information of government institutes such as military and diplomat information. Such networks have large and diverse attack surfaces, creating wide possibilities for attackers to sneak in.

The old-fashioned method of protecting enterprise networks was to deploy firewalls on the network perimeter, thus isolating internal trusted networks holding enterprise data and applications from the dangers of the outside unsecured network (in other words, the Internet). This defense model was common ten years ago, but with the explosive growth of Internet communications and mobile device technology, enterprises are no longer operating in their premises only. Nowadays, most enterprises grant remote access into their internal network to remote employees, partners, and contractors. Obviously, this makes securing the perimeter only an obsolete solution as intruders can now surpass the perimeter security (the traditional firewall) and infect endpoint devices directly (e.g., when an unsuspecting employee opens a malicious e-mail attachment on their workstation).

The new model of communication where remote users (whether they are customers or employees) access the internal corporate network and use its applications opens the door for all types of malicious attacks and malware. To counter this threat, enterprises

© Nihad A. Hassan 2019
N. A. Hassan, *Ransomware Revealed*, https://doi.org/10.1007/978-1-4842-4255-1_5

need to implement a new type of defense strategy that does not focus solely on securing the gateway of their network but also secures endpoint devices, servers, networking devices, and data, without forgetting to implement security awareness training for their end users. Such a comprehensive multilayered defense strategy is known as a *defense-in-depth* (DiD) strategy.

DiD is a cybersecurity defense strategy where multiple layers of defenses are deployed to protect enterprise IT systems. If one defense fails, another layer steps up immediately to counter the attack. DiD architecture addresses different attack vectors and works to protect the entire IT system from both internal and external attacks.

In this chapter, I cover the main security elements that every organization should consider when protecting a network from malware attacks, focusing primarily on ransomware. According to many studies, outdated operating systems and applications are still the main sources of data breaches, so I start by talking about this issue.

Efficient Patch Management

Patch management is sometimes ignored in the computer security discipline, even though it should be the first element in any cybersecurity protection plan. To keep systems safe against ransomware and other malware types, enterprises should have a rigid patch management policy that clearly defines the patching controls and constraints to lower cyberthreats affecting enterprise IT systems.

As technology continues to evolve daily, keeping an IT system current requires commitment and planning. *Patch management* is the process of keeping your operating system, installed software, and other IT services current to prevent attackers from taking advantage of any security vulnerability that can compromise systems. Patching includes updating all enterprise digital asset devices, including the following: network devices (WiFi access points, routers, firewalls, intrusion detection systems [IDSs]), servers, PCs, laptops, printers, storage devices, phones, tablets, PDAs) and any Internet capable-device (Internet of Things [IoT] devices) in addition to OSs, installed applications, antivirus solutions, database systems, financial software, program components, and content management systems (CMSs).

Note!   According to a report titled "Today's State of Vulnerability Response: Patch Work Demands Attention" published by ServiceNow and the Ponemon Institute that addresses the importance of patch management, "57 percent of respondents who reported a breach said that they were breached due to a vulnerability for which a patch was available but not applied. 34 percent say they actually knew they were vulnerable before the breach occurred."[1]

Patching cannot happen in a few clicks; the people responsible for patching IT assets need first to identify the needed updates/patches (the patch is simply a piece of code). After that, they should install and test these patches on nonproduction machines (e.g., virtualized environments). Finally, they can implement these updates on the production systems and document them.

The following are the main components of any general patch management policy:

- All IT devices and software applications and OSs need to be updated and patched to prevent any security exploit.

- Patching should include all Internet-capable devices, networking devices, OSs, all installed software and third-party applications, device firmware, and all information systems within an organization.

- Patches should be tested first on nonproduction devices before being applied on production systems.

- Noncritical patches should be applied during the maintenance time.

- Critical data should be backed up before applying any new patch.

- If there is an exception for not deploying a patch (e.g., legacy systems, fear of instability, and/or downtime), the patch manager should justify this and raise the issue to the information security department.

[1]Servicenow, "Today's State of Vulnerability Response: Patch Work Demands Attention," April 25, 2019 https://www.servicenow.com/content/dam/servicenow-assets/public/en-us/doc-type/resource-center/analyst-report/ponemon-state-of-vulnerability-response.pdf

- Remote users connected to an organization's IT systems must adhere to the patch management policy when updating and patching their devices so their devices become as secure as the enterprise-managed devices.

- For remote users, a patch policy can include a list of forbidden software that users cannot install on their endpoint devices.

- Deployed patches should be documented.

- Regular updating of a patch policy is a must to stay in line with governance and other regulatory compliance bodies.

Patch Management Tools

Patching all your IT devices manually is a daunting task, especially if you need to deploy these updates to hundreds of endpoint devices and servers with different OSs. You can automate the patching process by using different tools. The following are the most popular ones (all these tools are commercial):

- Microsoft System Center Configuration Manager (SCCM, (`https://www.microsoft.com/en-us/cloud-platform/system-center-configuration-manager-licensing`)

- Windows Patch Management (`https://www.itarian.com/patch-management/windows-patch-management.php`, currently free)

- SolarWinds Patch Manager (`https://www.solarwinds.com`)

- Ivanti Patch (`https://www.ivanti.com/solutions/security`)

Note!   Windows has a built-in patching utility for deploying the latest Microsoft product updates called Windows Server Update Services (WSUS). It is available on all Windows Server OSs, but its main disadvantage is that it deals only with Microsoft products.

Harden Your Environment

In this section, I make recommendations for hardening your enterprise IT environment, making it more resistant to ransomware infection.

Physical Security

The security of digital assets (server, workstation, backup storage, networking facilities, and so on) has equal importance to the data stored within them. In computer security, the precautionary measures that restrict access to facilities, equipment, and resources are known as *physical security*. For example, a malicious actor can surpass all software security controls (e.g., antivirus, firewall, IDS) and spread ransomware across the enterprise network if they succeed in gaining physical access (e.g., plugging in a malicious USB) to an endpoint device or to a server machine. These are some tips to assure the physical security of computing equipment:

- Restrict access to your facility using access control systems such as a keycard or biometric system.

- Use CCTV systems to monitor your facility remotely; cameras should cover all sensitive areas clearly.

- Restrict access to server rooms and to any area within your facility holding sensitive equipment. Only authorized IT personnel should have access to such areas.

- Do not allow your employees to leave their endpoint devices (laptop, workstation, or tablet) unattended. Ask your employees to turn off their device or to lock its screen with a password when they are away.

- Keep data storage media such as external hard drives, USB drives, CD/DVDs, and any backup media out of sight. A central storage server should be stored in the locked server room.

- Disconnect unused endpoints from your networks; such machines can be exploited in different ways to compromise your IT system.

- Portable end-user computing devices (e.g., tablets, laptops, smartphones) should be stored in a locked cabinet when not in use.

- Do not connect visitors' computing devices to your network, and do not give them access to your WiFi access point.

- Enforce physical security rules on all visitors to your premises. For instance, visitors or contractors should wear a badge to indicate their work and the areas they are authorized to enter within the facility.

Having physical security measures will help you prevent unauthorized access to your network and to your enterprise premises.

Network Segmentation

Network segmentation is an effective countermeasure to fight against ransomware as it lowers the impact of network intrusion and makes it hard for an adversary to find and access the segment where sensitive information is stored.

In network segmentation, you split a large network into smaller segments using firewalls, routers, virtual local area networks (VLANs), and other network separation techniques. In addition to isolating sensitive data in secure segments, network segmentation will increase the time needed for attackers to discover and map target network after the intrusion, making them more susceptible to discovery by firewalls and intrusion detection systems.

Without network segmentation, if ransomware successfully compromises an endpoint, it can propagate to all other endpoints connected to the same network (see Figure 5-1).

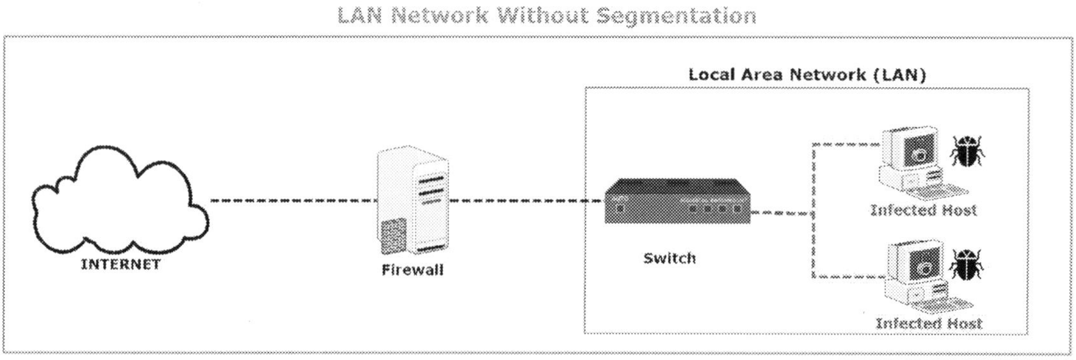

Figure 5-1. *In a flat network topology, infecting one endpoint will propagate the infection to all endpoints connected to the same LAN network*

By segmenting a network, traffic between different segments will pass through a firewall. This allows you to install a dedicated anti-ransomware solution at the connection point to stop ransomware propagation between different network segments (see Figure 5-2).

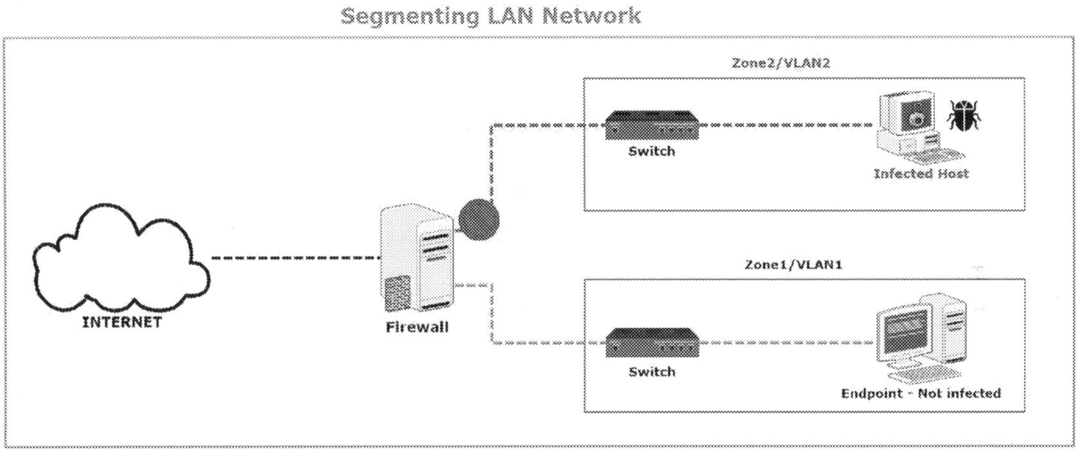

Figure 5-2. *Separating LAN into segments prevents ransomware infection from propagating to other segments*

Deploy a Generic Anti-ransomware Product

Having an antivirus solution is not enough to stop ransomware attacks. There are many specialized anti-ransomware products on the market today, and having a dedicated solution that protects both servers and endpoints from ransomware attacks provides an additional layer of defense to protect your network. The best anti-ransomware solutions use behavior analysis and cloud-based detection to detect and stop ransomware. These detection techniques surpass the signature-based detection methods that are still employed by most typical antivirus programs. While antivirus programs focus on capturing malware at an early stage, anti-ransomware programs have specialized features to fight against ransomware infection that traditional antivirus programs do not offer, such as preventing ransomware from completing its encryption routine, monitoring file manipulation operations, executing suspicious files in a virtual environment (sandboxing), and taking a real-time backup of critical files and storing the backup in secure containers if a suspected ransomware attack is underway.

Anti-ransomware programs are commercial, so I will not recommend any product; however, make sure to compare the features of different vendors, read previous customer reviews, and check the license agreement before buying a solution.

Use Least-Privilege Accounts

As mentioned in the previous chapter, use limited-privilege accounts for your employees' daily work. Even the IT administrators should use the nonprivileged account during their daily work unless they are performing an IT task that requires administrative privileges. In this case, they should use a secondary privileged account. The most common places to enforce the least-privilege model is on endpoint devices and network shares.

Vulnerability Management

According to the International Organization for Standardization (ISO), a *vulnerability* is "a weakness of an asset or group of assets that can be exploited by one or more threats." From a cybersecurity perspective, a vulnerability is a weakness in software programs that allows malicious actors to compromise a computer system.

Vulnerability management is the practice of identifying vulnerabilities in computer systems and then working to remove the risks before they get exploited by a malicious actor. Having a vulnerability management program is essential for every organization wanting to protect its IT systems from cyberattacks.

There are commonly four stages of any vulnerability management program.

- **Discovery**: List all IT assets (both hardware and software) within your organization. Having an IT inventory management program will simplify this task.

- **Reporting**: Use a vulnerability scanner program to scan your IT devices and then report the vulnerabilities found for each one.

- **Prioritization**: Rank discovered vulnerabilities according to each one's risk.

- **Response**: Implement remediation to close these vulnerabilities starting with the most critical one.

Vulnerability Scanning Tools

To detect vulnerabilities and patch them properly, you need to scan your networks, computer devices, and applications to find them. Table 5-1 lists the most popular vulnerability scanning tools along with each one's license type.

Table 5-1. *Vulnerability Scanner Programs*

Tool Name	Web Site	License Type
Nessus	`https://www.tenable.com/products/nessus/nessus-professional`	Commercial
Tripwire IP360	`https://www.tripwire.com/products/tripwire-ip360`	Commercial
OpenVAS	`http://www.openvas.org`	Free
Wireshark	`https://www.wireshark.org`	Free
Aircrack	`https://www.aircrack-ng.org`	Free
Nikto	`https://www.cirt.net/Nikto2`	Free
Nexpose Community	`https://www.rapid7.com/info/nexpose-community`	Free

Note!   A vulnerability scan should be performed frequently to avoid leaving the system vulnerable for a long period of time. A monthly scan is preferred for big organizations.

Next-Generation Firewalls

Up to now, any network security protection plan starts with installing a firewall at the network perimeter. Traditional firewall solutions, which use packet filtering through port/protocol inspection, are no longer adequate to stop modern malware attacks. The continual changes in application usage, threat landscape, user behavior, and the increasingly complex infrastructures of today's network environments require adopting new firewall solutions that use packet content inspection (among other advanced features) to identify application traffic regardless of port, protocol, or encryption used.

Firewalls come in two shapes: software and hardware. Small companies (ten employees or fewer) may prefer to install a software solution. However, managing it is a daunting task, as you need to install a firewall on each device. A hardware firewall is preferable over the software counterpart and needs less administrative work. Please note that the hardware firewall is not only a hardware piece, as it needs software components to do its work.

For most enterprises (even the small one), the ideal solution is to have a hardware firewall installed on the network perimeter. Modern firewalls known as *next-generation firewall*s (NGFWs) come bundled with advanced security tools like antivirus, anti-malware, and antispam tools, and they support virtual private network (VPN) connections in addition to all the capabilities of traditional firewall technology.

Using an NGFW firewall, network administrators can identify applications and enforce a network security policy to prevent unauthorized applications from passing traffic (e.g., apply an application's blacklist and whitelist), in addition to blocking any protocol they find risky and closing all network ports when they are not in use to prevent port scanning tools from discovering open ports. For example, RDP, which has been exploited by many ransomware strains, can be blocked entirely across the network via a firewall.

Note!   If your users need RDP access, make sure they connect over a secure VPN.

Many firewall vendors offer NGFW devices that come bundled with intrusion prevention systems and advanced anti-malware capabilities that use signature- and heuristic-based detection. Some NGFW products integrate with Active Directory to apply firewall application usage rules on individual users and groups in Windows environments (this feature is known as *identity awareness*). NGFWs can strengthen enterprise network defenses against ransomware attacks.

Intrusion Detection Systems and Intrusion Prevention Systems

Like firewalls, intrusion detection systems (IDSs) and intrusion prevention systems (IPSs) come either as hardware devices (with software components) or as software applications. Both IDSs and IPSs inspect network traffic for signatures that match a database of known cyberattacks signatures. However, they differ in the action they take when malicious activity is detected.

IDSs come in two types: network and host-based. Obviously, a network IDS will monitor network traffic, while a host-based intrusion detection system (HIDS) installs on individual computers and actively monitors the state of a system (e.g., file integrity checks, log analysis, process monitoring, Windows registry monitoring, detecting malicious software launched from USB devices) and the network traffic passing through its network interfaces.

IDSs monitor network traffic without taking any protective measures. When a potential incident is detected, it fires an alarm (or sends a notification) so that another system or a human can perform an action such as closing the attack entry point or reconfiguring the firewall to stop future attacks.

Note!   Ossec (`https://www.ossec.net`) is a free open source intrusion detection system.

An intrusion prevention system does similar work to an IDS in monitoring network traffic but acts differently when detecting malicious activity. An IPS uses deep packet inspection and proactively monitors network traffic for suspicious activity and takes preventative action automatically (e.g., denying malicious traffic) to deter the attack. Unlike an IDS, which does not take automatic countermeasures, an IPS is a control system that prevents and allows packet delivery using a predefined policy. The cyberattack signature database is the main component of any IPS/IDS system; it contains known attack patterns and protocol anomalies and should be updated periodically to prevent newly discover cyberthreats from passing in. For example, in a ransomware attack case, an IPS can stop exploit kit code before reaching the target endpoint. An IPS can also block the connection with command-and-control (C&C) servers if any of the endpoints get infected with ransomware (post-infection).

Many IDS/IPS vendors are now integrating newer IPSs with firewalls to create a unified threat management (UTM) technology. UTM combines the security functions of all these solutions in one appliance at a single point on the network. UTM brings the following protection to enterprise networks:

- UTM provides antivirus, anti-malware, and antispam capabilities, in addition to scanning all incoming e-mail attachments.

- By using an IPS, known attacks can be stopped before reaching the internal network.

- UTM provides web filtering to prevent access to unwanted web sites.

- UTM provides content filtering based on the file MIME type, file extension, or protocol type, in addition to blocking other content like ActiveX, Java applets, and Flash objects as required.

- UTM incorporates data leak prevention (DLP) technology.

- UTM updates its IPS cyberthreats signature database in addition to other security solutions virus definition lists (antivirus and antimalware) automatically without any user intervention.

- Network security administrators can manage a wide range of security tools using one management console.

Note!   Utilizing UTM for network defense should not make us abandon other security products (e.g., installing antivirus software on endpoint devices). Using a single device to protect the entire IT infrastructure goes against a DiD strategy, which suggests protecting computer networks with a series of defense layers.

The UTM and NGFW terms are often used synonymously by both customers and vendors. They share common functions; however, they are different in terms of customization and simplicity. For instance, UTM is easier to administer and deploy, making it a preferred solution for small to medium-sized businesses, while NGFW is more suitable for large enterprises wanting to customize their security policies and who have adequate resources and security expertise to manage different security appliances.

Network Sandboxing

Next-gen firewalls use signatures and heuristic detection methods with great success to block malware attacks. However, with an ever-increasing number of threats, such detection methods are not enough, especially when countering zero-day threats or targeted attacks.

I talked about sandboxing technology previously. On the network side, sandboxing is increasingly becoming an important security layer at the network perimeter. Network sandboxing works by sending suspicious files into an isolated virtual environment (sandbox) to examine its code. If the subject file is found malicious, it will get terminated; otherwise, it will be marked as legitimate and be allowed to pass the network perimeter.

Many NGFW vendors offer a cloud sandboxing feature on a subscription basis, where suspicious files are sent to the cloud infrastructure to analyze its behaviors when executed. With the continual increase in ransomware attacks, network sandboxing is an essential component of network defense to protect against all threats, both known and unknown, before entering the internal network. You should assure that your future firewall supports the sandboxing feature.

Note!   Next-gen firewalls can combine IPS/IDS and network sandboxing in one unit. Always consult the firewall feature list before buying one.

Warning!   The sandboxing technique still has some limitations. Malware authors are continually improving their code to create "sandbox-aware" malware that can detect if it is being executed in a sandbox; if so, the malware will behave differently so it will not be flagged as malicious.

Malicious URL Blocking

After ransomware successfully infects a system, it needs to communicate with its C&C servers to receive instructions and to prorogate to other computers within the infected network. Blocking access to malicious domains is an effective countermeasure to stop both ransomware infection and spread. For instance, firewalls and IPSs can be configured to block ransomware botnet C&C traffic. There are many web sites that offer lists of known malware and phishing sites that can be imported into the firewall to terminate the connection to malicious sites. The following are the most popular ones:

- **Ransomware tracker** (`https://ransomwaretracker.abuse.ch/blocklist`): This offers updated lists of blocklists to block ransomware botnet C&C traffic.

- **aa419** (`https://db.aa419.org/fakebankslist.php`): This lists fraudulent web sites.

- **Malc0de Database** (`http://malc0de.com/database`): This lists sites with malicious content.

- **Malware Domain** (`https://www.malwaredomainlist.com`): A malicious URL domain list.

- **DNS-BH** (`http://www.malwaredomains.com/wordpress/?page_id=66`): This contains malware domain blocklists.

- **Open Phish** (`https://openphish.com`): This lists thousands of phishing sites daily.

Tip!   Using a central proxy server to restrict access to sites and online services of all computers that have Internet access across an organization's network is a must-have countermeasure against phishing and other malicious sites. Most antivirus programs have web filtering and blocking capabilities that can be configured to restrict access to malicious sites on endpoint devices also.

You should consider blocking access to the TOR network (The Onion Router). Many ransomware strains use the TOR network as a communication channel with its C&C server. The `https://www.dan.me.uk/tornodes` web site offers a list of TOR nodes (including EXIT nodes) and is updated each 30 minutes.

Blocking access to the TOR nodes is not enough to prevent your users and possible malware from accessing the TOR network completely. Consider the following measures:

- Create security rules within your firewall to prevent the following applications from accessing the Internet (tor, tor2web, ssh, ssh-tunnel, like, IPsec-esp, http-proxy).

- Use application filters to block applications based on their behavior and deny all unknown applications.

- Create a security policy (whitelisting) to prevent the execution of TOR software on endpoint devices.

Create Honeypots

A *honeypot* is a computer system trap used to mislead cybercriminals when trying to gain unauthorized access to information systems. A honeypot announces itself online as a potential high-value target (e.g., file or database server) for cybercriminals. Enterprises use honeypots to detect or deflect intruders from attacking the real systems. A honeypot is also used by cybersecurity research centers to understand how new cyberattacks are developed and to learn more about the new attacking techniques employed by cybercriminals to do their malicious activities (see Figure 5-3).

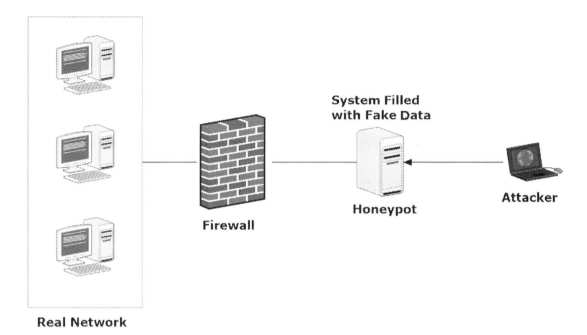

Figure 5-3. *Honeypot security*

To protect against ransomware, an enterprise can set up a fake server (the honeypot) and fill it with unimportant files. If ransomware successfully compromises the honeypot machine, the system administrator will get notified to take the necessary action (e.g., terminating the session of the user or machine that is hosting the attacking ransomware).

By checking the honeypot logs and monitoring the network traffic to such systems, security administrators can understand the behavior of cybercriminals and the techniques employed by them to penetrate systems. The most important value of honeypot systems is examining the effectiveness of the applied security measures and knowing which one is not functioning properly to improve it.

Network Performance Baseline

A network performance baseline is a set of network metrics taken under normal operating conditions of the organization network and used by network administrators to compare the baseline with the current network traffic to identify any security breach or application problems.

Monitoring unusual network activity can reveal advanced cyberattacks like advanced persistent threats (APTs) and ransomware. For example, having traffic originated from an endpoint device -that is usually used to access the internet and CRM server only- to other endpoints and to the file storage server may indicate a ransomware attack trying to spread across the enterprise network, in such a case, quarantining the infected endpoint can stop the attack spread.

Note!   Keeping network logs for at least one year is recommended to have evidence in case your countermeasures lead to a criminal investigation.

E-mail Security

As mentioned in Chapter 2, e-mail is the number-one vehicle for delivering ransomware and is considered the preferred gateway for intruders to gain access to an organization's network. A research conducted by IBM in 2017 concluded that 59 percent of ransomware attacks comes via phishing e-mails, and 91 percent of all malware is delivered via e-mail systems.

There are different types of e-mail attacks, however, from a ransomware attack perspective. E-mail can be utilized to infect systems with ransomware through two methods.

- Spam/phishing e-mails try to convince a user to click links within the e-mail body that contain malicious files (e.g., PDFs, ZIP files, Word documents, or JavaScript) or lead to a compromised web site housing an exploit kit.

- Malicious e-mails hold ransomware as an attachment.

In this section, I talk about the needed security measures that should be implemented by any organization to protect its network from ransomware delivered via e-mail. I defer talking about end-user e-mail security until the next chapter because it is considered part of end-user cybersecurity awareness training.

Advanced E-mail Spam Filtering

An e-mail spam message is an unsolicited message sent via e-mail systems without the receiver's consent. Spam is not only annoying for the receiver; it can also be dangerous when spammers send e-mails with malicious attachments or contain links to malicious destinations.

More than half of e-mails sent worldwide is believed to be spam, according to Statista's article "Spam messages accounted for 57 percent of e-mail traffic in December 2018."[2] The main intent of spam e-mails is for advertising purposes, but a large volume comes with harmful content. The following are some methods to lower the amount of spam messages received:

- **Filter by content**: Apply content filters (by supplying words) to prevent spam e-mails from reaching endpoint devices. The filtering mechanism can take place on a gateway (e.g., enterprise e-mail server), in a third-party spam filter that can be integrated into the enterprise's own devices or in the cloud, or on the end user's computer.

- **IP address filtering**: Spam e-mails can also be filtered according to sender IP address.

- **Prevent e-mail harvesting**: Spammers use different e-mail harvesting techniques to collect e-mail addresses in bulk from web pages to use them later in their spam campaigns. E-mail harvesting can be avoided using different techniques.

  - Obfuscate your e-mail address to make it readable for humans but difficult to capture by automated bots. For example, use "nihad at darknessgate dot com" (nihad@darknessgate.com). Another technique to obfuscate e-mail addresses (that is too difficult to detect by bots) is to use an e-mail schema and post it online. For example, a company can denote the following e-mail schema on its web site: "[Last Name].[First Name]@darknessgate.com."

  - Embed e-mail addresses into images and post them online. It is too difficult for bots read text inside the image.

---

[2]https://www.statista.com/statistics/420391/spam-email-traffic-share

- **Use contact forms**: By using a contact form, the recipient's e-mail address will be hidden in the back-end code of the web page.

- **Use a disposable e-mail address**: People should not use their private or work e-mail address to register with some free online services or to receive online offers (e.g., download free e-books) to avoid exposing their real e-mail to spammers. If you want to provide your e-mail address to a site you do not trust, it is advisable to use a temporary e-mail address that can be configured to last for a specific period (e.g., hours or even minutes). There are many sites that offer such a service like Guerrilla Mail (`https://www.guerrillamail.com`) and TempMail (`https://temp-mail.org/en`)

- **Disable HTML in receiving e-mails**: Reading your e-mail in plain text is an effective solution to preventing scripts embedded in links and images from executing as soon as you open the e-mail. It is also advisable to disable the e-mail preview window and "disallow remote content" in the opened message in your e-mail client (see Figure 5-4).

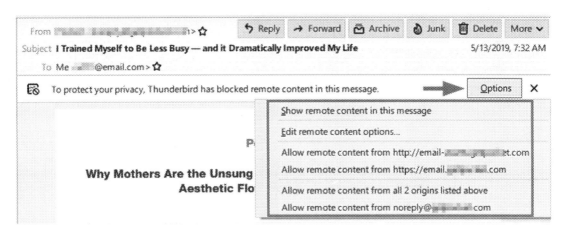

Figure 5-4. *Viewing remote content using the Thunderbird e-mail client*

- Enterprises should consider using technologies such as Sender Policy Framework (SPF), Domain-based Message Authentication Reporting and Conformance (DMARC), and DomainKeys Identified Mail (DKIM) to stop spam and other types of phishing e-mails from entering their network. For instance, SPF is an e-mail authentication technique that prevents spammers from sending spoofed e-mails using your domain name. SPF works by checking the IP address of the sender to make sure it is authorized by the sending domain name. DMARC is a technology based on SPF for preventing cybercriminals from using your domain name for sending spam and phishing e-mails. DKIM standard is like SPF; however, instead of using the sender IP address to validate the e-mail authenticity, it uses a digital signature to associate a domain name with its claimed e-mail message; DKIM works by attaching the digital signature of a domain name with each outgoing e-mail message sent using it.

Block Attachments

One of the most common ways to infect with ransomware is via file attachments. To protect against this risk, it is advisable to configure your e-mail server to block certain types of files that are considered risky.

If your enterprise sets a policy of blocking dangerous file types sent via e-mails and you want to send a blocked file type, you can use cloud storage to upload the blocked file and then send the download link to the recipient or simply rename the file (change its extension) before sending it to surpass the restriction.

WARNING! LIST OF FILE EXTENSIONS THAT SHOULD NOT BE OPENED WHEN SENT AS AN E-MAIL ATTACHMENT

Most computer users think that executable files (with an `.exe` extension) are the only dangerous file type that they should avoid opening when received through e-mail. Unfortunately, this information is not complete, as there are a large number of file types that can be used to execute malicious code. The following are the most dangerous file formats that you should not open when sent as an attachment:

EXE, MSI, MSP, PIF, APPLICATION, GADGET, HTA , CPL, MSC, JAR, CMD, VB, VBS, VBE, JSE, PS1, PS2, MSH, MSH1, MSH2, MSHXML, SCF, LNK, INF, REG, JS WSC, WSH

Microsoft Office files can contain malicious code in the form of macros. If an Office document extension ends with an `.m`, it can contain macros (e.g., `.docm`, `.xlsm`, and `.pptm`). Be careful to not run Office macros sent from unknown senders.

Finally, do not open zip files protected with passwords (a password is usually sent in the body of the e-mail). Attackers use this trick to prevent antivirus software from investigating the encrypted compressed file, which can contain malware ready to launch after being opened.

Implement a Data Classification Policy

A data classification policy helps an organization to categorize its digital data assets (e.g., files, databases, etc.) into groups, giving each group a special access permission and storage location. This will effectively lower the organization's overall risks by focusing the protection effort on safeguarding the most critical data.

Data can be classified at the time of creation using simple methods such as inserting a classification tag into the file's metadata (see Figure 5-5) or using a dedicated data classification solution, which is more appealing to large enterprises. Classifying data will help an organization determine the best security controls needed to protect its data.

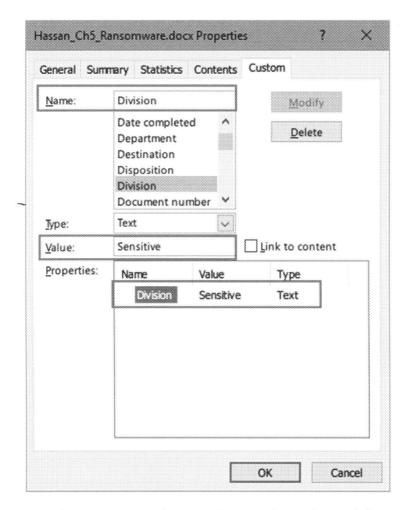

Figure 5-5. *Inserting a new metadata tag into a Microsoft Word document to categorize a subject file as Sensitive*

Enforce Strong Password Requirements

People's choice of passwords continues to pose a huge security risk. Make sure to enforce strong passwords on your users to protect their accounts when using remote management services and file sharing tools. Here are some tips to create secure passwords:

- The password should be at least 15 characters in length.

- The password should contain at least one lowercase letter, one uppercase letter, one number, and one symbol (e.g., #, %, &).

- The password shouldn't be your username, your spouse's, family member names (including your name), or your pet's name or any part of it.

- Do not use your gender or birth date/place as part of your password.

- Do not the same password for two accounts (have two e-mails with the same password).

- Do not use place names or famous people's names for your password.

- Change your password once every month and do not use the same password again.

- Do not let your web browser save your entered passwords.

- Implement two-factor authentication where applicable.

- Use a password manager to organize and protect your passwords such as KeePass Password Safe (`https://keepass.info`) and Password Safe (`https://pwsafe.org`).

- Use password generation tools to create strong, complex passwords that can be difficult or impossible to crack using brute-force, dictionary, or guessing attacks. Password manager programs have a built-in password generation feature; you can also use a dedicated program for this purpose such as PWGen (`http://pwgen-win.sourceforge.net`).

Implement a Software Usage Restriction Policy

Installing security solutions for endpoints and network perimeters is not enough to protect against ransomware attacks. You should have another line of defense in case ransomware succeeds in reaching to endpoint devices. Application whitelisting is a proactive technique to prevent all types of applications (any executable file) from executing on end-user machines. In such a scenario, only a small set of applications defined by the IT administrator can run by default; all other applications are forbidden. Obviously, such a restriction is considered the most effective measure for defending against unknown malware that has not been discovered yet in addition to other threats that exploit zero-day vulnerabilities to sneak in.

In Windows environments, there are two built-in security mechanisms to implement application control policies across the enterprise: SRP and AppLocker. By controlling which executable code is allowed or prohibited from running on an endpoint, enterprises can significantly improve security by preventing unknown malware, including ransomware, from executing on endpoint devices.

In the previous chapter, I talked about SRP, which can be configured to work on both local and domain machines, and how you can use it to create a restrictive Windows environment to control the execution of untrusted applications and scripts. In this chapter, I cover the second security mechanism for application whitelisting, introduced with recent versions of Windows (beginning in certain editions of Windows 7), named AppLocker.

Note!   Windows has a third security mechanism for application whitelisting named Windows Defender Application Control (WDAC). WDAC comes with more advanced features than SRP and AppLocker. For example, it can block executable files on the kernel level and implement application whitelisting more strictly. In addition, starting from Windows 10 version 1703, WDAC can be configured to control which add-ins are allowed/prohibited from running in a specific application. WDAC is mostly used in an enterprise context where the IT department specifies which applications can run on endpoint devices according to an enterprise's predefined security policy.

Windows AppLocker

Microsoft released AppLocker as the next generation of the SRP technology; it comes with many enhancements that surpass SRP, such as the following:

- It can assign a rule to specific users/groups.

- Separate rules can be defined for each type of executable file (e.g., a rule for installers and another for scripts).

- It has an audit mode so you can test the policy before enforcing it.

- You can export applied rules to XML so you can use them somewhere else.

AppLocker restricts executables based on the following four types of rules: path rules, file hash rules, publisher rules, and packaged app rules. Like SRP, AppLocker can be configured both on a local machine (using Local Group Policy Editor) or in Group Policy (using Group Policy Management Console).

To configure AppLocker on a local machine using Windows 10, do the following:

1. Go to the Windows Start menu and type **gpedit.msc** to launch the Windows Group Policy Editor.

2. Navigate to Computer Configuration ➤ Windows Settings ➤ Security Settings ➤ Application Control Policies ➤ AppLocker and select "Configure rule enforcement" (see Figure 5-6).

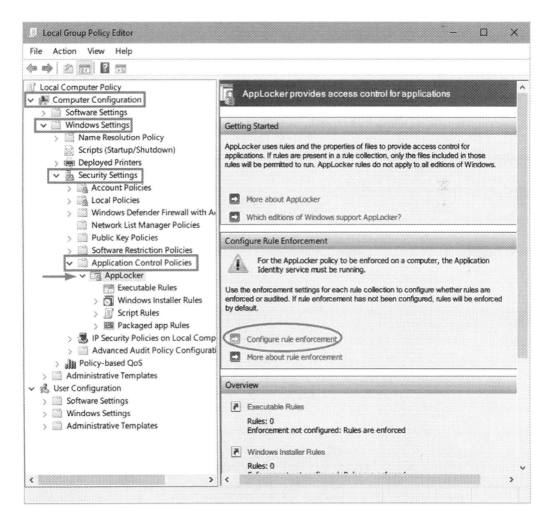

Figure 5-6. *Accessing AppLocker configuration settings on Windows 10*

3. Select Configured under "Executable rules" and then click OK
   (see Figure 5-7).

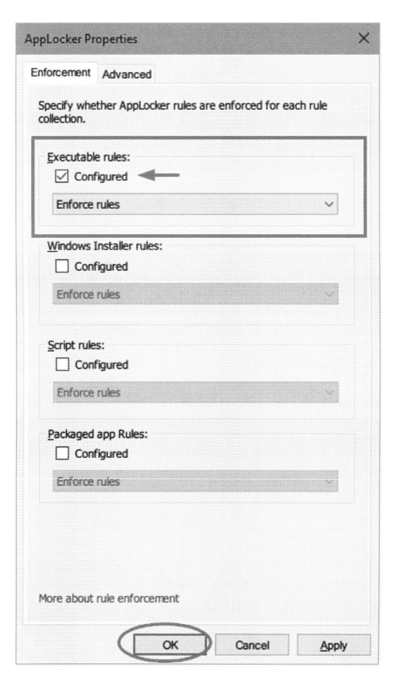

Figure 5-7. *Accessing AppLocker rule enforcement properties; in my case, I'm creating rules for executable applications*

4. Right-click Executable Rules under AppLocker in the left pane and then click Automatically Generate Rules (see Figure 5-8).

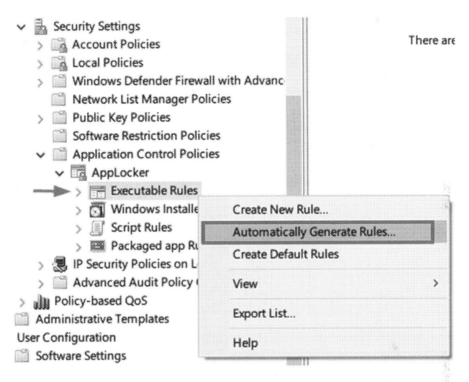

Figure 5-8. *Automatically generating application rules for all executables using AppLocker*

Note!   Select Create Default Rules (Figure 5-8) to create default rules where users are only allowed to run applications under `C:\Program Files` or Windows folders.

---

5. A new window appears where you can select the folder that contains the applications you want to allow to execute. Type a name to identify this set of rules (see Figure 5-9). Click Next to continue.

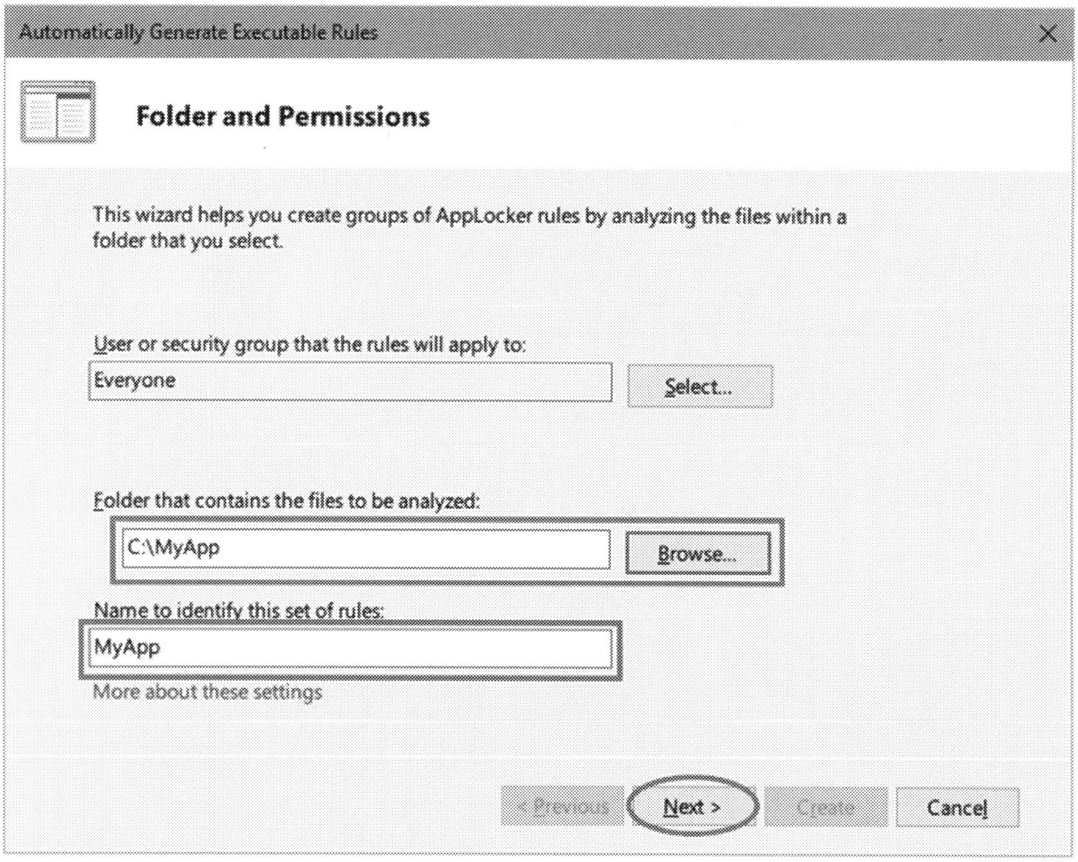

Figure 5-9. *Selecting the folder that contains the applications you want to permit to run and giving a name to identify this set of rules*

6. The Rule Preferences window comes next (see Figure 5-10). Leave the default options as they are, and click Next to continue.

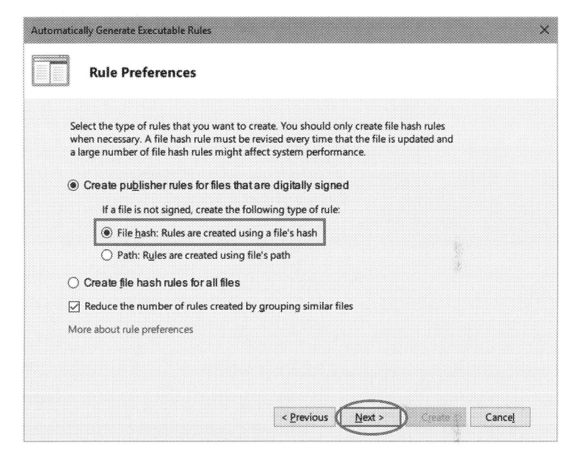

Figure 5-10. *The default settings in Rule Preferences should be OK*

7. AppLocker may need some time to generate all the rules according to the number of applications in the specified folder. After finishing, the Review Rules page appears; click the Create button to create the specified rules and close the wizard.

8. A pop-up message appears (see Figure 5-11); hit Yes to continue.

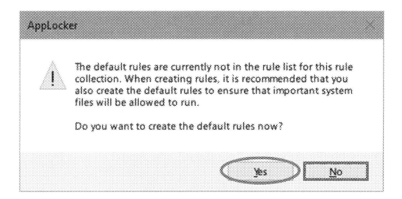

Figure 5-11. *Creating default rules by clicking Yes so that important system files can still run (allow executing applications in the Windows and Program Files folders)*

    9.   The rules will appear in the right pane of the Executable Rules option (see Figure 5-12)

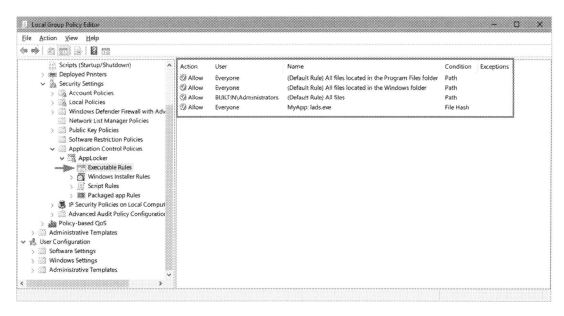

Figure 5-12. *The first three rules are the default rules, and the last one is the folder specified that contains the whitelisted applications*

10.   If you want to change the user or user groups that a specific rule applies to, right-click the rule and select Properties (see Figure 5-13).

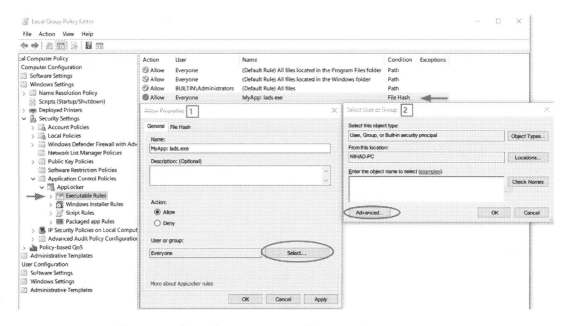

Figure 5-13.   *Changing the rule assignment for users/user groups*

11.   Finally, before AppLocker will enforce the rules, the Application Identity service must be started on each device. To start the Application Identity service, go to Administrative Tools ➤ Services ➤ Application identity and click the Start button. Make sure to change the startup type to Automatic.

12.   Restart the device and you are done!

NOTES ABOUT USING APPLOCKER

- AppLocker application control is intended to apply to Standard users, not Administrator accounts.

- AppLocker must be used in conjunction with the User Account Control (UAC).

- Make sure to install the default required programs for your work in the C:\Program Files or C:\Program Files (x86) folders.

This was a quick introduction to configuring AppLocker to control application execution. Deploying an application whitelisting technology such as AppLocker will effectively help enterprises lower security risks when an unsuspecting user executes malicious software inadvertently.

DNS Security

I already covered different security solutions and services to block malware, ransomware, and other malicious web sites (e.g., phishing web sites). However, as mentioned, one solution is not enough to mitigate such threats. The preferred approach is to have multiple lines of defense to stop these attacks and use secure DNS servers for both individual and corporate use. This will add an additional layer of protection to your defense against ransomware.

Ransomware utilizes the Domain Name System (DNS) at different stages of an attack. For example, DNS reconnaissance is used during targeted attacks to gain insight about the target enterprise's network such as subdomains and web hosts. DNS is also used in the delivery process of e-mail spam campaigns that carry ransomware. Many ransomware strains need to use DNS to communicate with a C&C server. Therefore, using secure DNS servers to block malicious activities is crucial to mitigate, detect, and respond to such attacks more quickly.

There are different DNS-based threat blocking providers that offer protection against malware, ransomware, and have anti-phishing capabilities. The following are the most popular ones:

- OpenDNS (`https://www.opendns.com`), 208.67.222.222 to 208.67.220.220

- Comodo (`https://www.comodo.com/secure-dns`), 8.26.56.26 to 8.20.247.20

- Yandex.DNS (`https://dns.yandex.com/advanced`), 77.88.8.88 to 77.88.8.2

- Quad9 (`https://www.quad9.net`), 9.9.9.9

Enterprises should consider having a secure in-house DNS server or subscribing to a commercial threat-blocking DNS service with more advanced capabilities than the free providers for maximum protection.

Warning!   Beware that DNS providers can intercept all your web browsing history. For mission-critical tasks in an enterprise, consider deploying a self-hosted threat-blocking DNS server.

Data Sanitization

E-mail attachments and files downloaded from the Internet are commonly used as a vehicle to carry malicious code. Data sanitization (also known as *content disarm and reconstruction* [CDR]) is a protective anti-malware technology that assumes all files entering the enterprise network are malicious and that works to sanitize each file (removing potentially malicious code) before passing it to the endpoint device. Utilizing a data sanitization system at all entry points such as for e-mail attachments, for web browser downloads, and even on endpoint computers to sanitize files carried within USB devices is an essential protection measure against unknown malware and other advanced attacks exploiting zero-day vulnerabilities.

Note!   According to Gartner, "As malware sandbox evasion techniques improve, the use of content disarm and reconstruction (CDR) at the e-mail gateway as a supplement or alternative to sandboxing will increase."[3]

Govern USB Drive Use

As mentioned in the previous chapter, it is recommended that you avoid plugging untrusted USB devices into your work or home machine. In an enterprise context, sometimes you'll need to use USB devices to transfer data from a less secure network to the file's server repository located in a trusted network. Using USB devices in enterprises cannot be banned completely; however, some security measures should be implemented first to mitigate risks associated with USB devices.

---

[3]Gartner," Advancing Your Anti-Phishing Program," May 19,2019 https://www.gartner.com/ imagesrv/media-products/pdf/mimecast/Mimecast-1-4QT9Y3H.pdf

- All USB devices should be scanned first for malware on an isolated machine before plugging them into the enterprise network.

- Avoid plugging USB devices directly into endpoint devices when you want to transfer files. Instead, upload the needed files from a user's USB device into a central file repository where you can access them via a network share.

- Enforce a USB usage policy. For instance, allow/prohibit using USB devices based on the employee role in the enterprise. Most staff does not need to carry executable applications with them, so such file types should be blocked. On the other hand, PDF and Microsoft Office files are commonly used as attack vectors to carry ransomware. Such file types are used widely in business organizations, so you should consider sanitizing such file types to remove any potentially malicious code before opening them on endpoint devices.

Maintain Effective Backup and Recovery Strategy

The most important safeguard against ransomware attacks is to have a robust backup and recovery strategy for enterprise data. Businesses should focus on backing up the most critical data for business functions. Backups should be stored on a separate system (e.g., separate network segment) that cannot be accessed online. Backup media (whether it is a network backup server or a removable drive) should not remain permanently attached to the system that was backed up to avoid infecting it in the case of a successful ransomware attack taking place. You should also consider having multiple copies of your backup (at least three copies, with one of them off-site).

A cloud backup can be considered a secure option because it is located off your network; however, you should avoid continually backing up data in real time to the cloud, as some ransomware strains have the capability to encrypt cloud backups. Remember, if a ransomware attack hits your network, you should consider stopping any backup immediately to avoid backing up encrypted data.

To conclude, the local backup server should be isolated from your normal operating environment and should connect to the network only during the backup period. The backup server should also have a hardened operating system (preferably a Linux variant), as Windows is known to be a common target for ransomware attacks. Data backups should be conducted hourly to the local backup server, and after that nightly to another remote backup server that remains online only during the backup; a third backup should be conducted weekly to a removable storage media (e.g., tape drive). The integrity of backup files should be verified continually to make sure all critical information has been backed up; it is also important to test the recovery process regularly to ensure high availability in case you need it.

Data Loss Prevention

Data loss prevention (DLP) is a technology used to prevent users from leaking or even destroying sensitive information outside an organization. The main aim of a DLP solution is to monitor data flow within an organization across all electronic communication channels such as e-mail, instant messaging, file transfer, web forms, portable USB drives, and any other means to stop information leakage outside an organization's network.

DLP works according to a predefined security policy set by an organization or by a regulatory compliance body such as HIPAA or GDPR. A DLP solution will detect any violation of enforced rules immediately and implement protective steps (e.g., sending an alert, encrypting data, or terminating the session) to prevent users from intentionally or accidentally leaking sensitive information.

A DLP monitors data in three states.

- *Data at rest* is when the data resides in storage units such as databases and file repository servers.

- *Data in transit* is when data moves across the corporate network and/or to external networks such as the Internet using e-mail, web forms, or the traffic generated by malicious software.

- *Data in use* is when data is processed at endpoint devices. A user can leak data using USB drives, e-mail, FTP, file transfers to the cloud, and so on.

The other main task of a DLP solution is to prevent data loss. In a ransomware attack, data is encrypted, and legitimate users are denied access to it. The recovery of encrypted data can be impossible in many instances (e.g., you cannot recover files encrypted with the NotPetya ransomware, even if you pay the ransom). This ransomware attack falls under data loss. DLP solutions can help against ransomware attacks by informing the IT administrator early about any unusual traffic or a change of stored data (e.g., begin encryption) and can alert the administrator to isolate the infected machine or network segment.

DLP relies on access rights and a data classification policy defined by an organization to enforce its rules on end users.

Tools to Measure the Effectiveness of Your Defenses

After you have installed all the necessary security solutions and followed all measures to stop ransomware and other malware types, it is advisable to continually test your defenses to measure their effectiveness against real threats and to close any new vulnerability. In this section, I will mention some tools and services for testing security software and other network defenses against real-world attacks.

- **Spyshelter** (`https://www.spyshelter.com/security-test-tool`): Tests the installed security software to check its effectiveness against information-stealing malware.

- **RanSim** (`https://www.knowbe4.com/ransomware-simulator`): Finds out how vulnerable your network is against ransomware and cryptomining attacks. Currently, it simulates 15 ransomware infection scenarios and one crypto-mining infection scenario.

- **Wicar** (`https://www.wicar.org/test-malware.html`): Tests your antivirus/anti-malware software.

- **Testmyav** (`https://testmyav.com`): Tests your installed antivirus software.

- **FortiGuard** (`https://www.geckoandfly.com/24644/test-antivirus-security`): Tests if your network security can catch malware hiding in a compressed file.

Enforce a Security Policy

I have covered nearly all kinds of security solutions and devices to protect against ransomware and other malware types such as antivirus products, firewalls, IPSs, antispam, sandboxing, DLP, and CDR. However, security tools are not enough to mitigate and stop ransomware attacks. Enforcing security policies within an organization is essential to protect it from both internal and external threats and to assure its compliance with various regulations.

A security policy is a set of rules and procedures enforced by an organization on its employees when using its IT systems to maintain the security of its IT assets and resources. Every person within an organization must understand their obligations to protect data and IT assets. A security policy should include penalties when someone fails to adhere to its regulations.

A security policy should be written in a simple style with minimum technical jargon and define in high-level terms the best security practices to safeguard organization data and the IT system from malicious actors and accidental disclosure of sensitive information. A policy should define its scope; for example, a policy can apply to all employees, contractors, and partners accessing the organization's IT system or visiting its physical facilities.

Major Elements of a Security Policy Document

The following are the most important areas that should be included in any security policy:

- **Password policy**: Defines requirements for creating strong passwords and utilizing them properly in terms of usage and storage.

- **E-mail usage policy**: Defines the rules and restrictions imposed on users when using the organization's e-mail system.

- **Internet usage policy**: Defines rules and guidelines for the appropriate usage of organization Internet access. (For example, before deploying a firewall solution, you need to know the organization Internet usage policy to enforce it through this device.)

- **Organization-owned mobile device policy**: Defines rules on the appropriate usage of organization-owned mobile devices.

- **Users-owned mobile device policy**: Defines the rules and limitations on employees connecting their own mobile devices to the organization's IT infrastructure.

- **Remote access policy**: Defines rules and restrictions when accessing an organization's IT system remotely. (For example, a user must connect over a secure VPN connection.)

- **Data privacy policy**: Defines employee responsibilities in maintaining the secrecy of client information in compliance with applied national and international regulations.

- **Social media usage policy**: Defines rules and limitations and provides guidelines for employees when posting content online, either as part of their work or as a private entity.

- **Data classification policy**: Defines rules for establishing a framework that classifies data into groups based on their sensitivity to organization work.

- **Data breach policy**: Defines how an organization will react (notification procedures) when a breach of data occurs in accordance with the applied laws.

- **Patch management policy**: Defines the patching (updating) controls and constraints to lower cyberthreats affecting an organization's IT system by keeping them current and up-to-date.

- **Vulnerability management policy**: Defines procedures to conduct regular scans of an organization's IT systems to discover vulnerabilities and work to fix them properly.

- **Data encryption policy**: Provides guidance on using encryption techniques and protocols to secure data at rest and in transit in accordance with state regulations.

- **Data disposal policy**: Provides guidelines for destroying sensitive/confidential data securely.

- **Physical security policy**: Defines access protocols for employees and visitors entering organization premises to prevent unauthorized people from obtaining sensitive data.

- **Security awareness training policy**: Defines the training requirements of employees in relation to IT security to maintain a high level of security awareness, so all staff know what data is most critical to their organization work and know how to protect it.

Why Do You Need a Security Policy?

A security policy is a major element for any organization operating in today's information age and wanting to secure its work environment from both internal and external threats. Regardless of the size of an organization, having a security policy is essential to addressing all possible security threats and to suggesting countermeasures before they occur. Every organization needs a security policy for the following reasons:

- A security policy helps an organization to identify the risk factors in its work. For example, using weak passwords can result in compromising employee e-mail accounts and consequently leaking sensitive information.

- It provides guidelines on the acceptable usage of the Internet, e-mail system, and other digital devices within an organization.

- It increases operation efficiency by following secure procedures to perform daily work. This will result in saving time and resources and eventually money!

- It helps organization employees become IT security literate, thus strengthening an organization defense against most prevalent cyberattacks like ransomware and other malware types.

- It increases revenue! An organization that has a strong security policy in place can gain more deals and partnership agreements, as it will posture itself in the market as a reliable entity that can protect other vendors' data when working with it.

- A security policy will also increase customers' confidence (e.g., assure the privacy of their personal data), making them more willing to do business with the organization.

- It can minimize internal threats like data leaks and corporate espionage because of the enforced security controls.

- Human error is still the number-one threat to any organization through phishing attacks. Enforcing a security policy will lower this risk, as there will be guidelines and penalties on any unacceptable behavior conducted by employees that can lead to data theft, information leaks, or malware infections.

- Finally, having a security policy will simplify compliance with state, federal, and international data protection and privacy regulations.

A security policy provides a framework for handling all the security aspects of an organization and for defining the rules that must be followed by all employees to protect an organization's IT asset. When drafting a security policy for an organization, consider current business functions, organization structure, organization culture, and available budget. Do not write something in your policy that you cannot enforce. For example, forbidding the use of USB devices in your corporate environment is worthless if you do not have the required technical tools to stop such devices.

Summary

No one is isolated from the risk of ransomware attacks. From the individual home user to SMBs up to the largest institutions and government agencies, ransomware attacks are increasing in complexity and are becoming more capable of exploiting network and system vulnerabilities. In this chapter, I covered the enterprise side of protection against ransomware and other malware attacks. Corporate and government networks have a large attack surface, and protecting it requires a comprehensive security plan that employs a defense-in-depth strategy where several defense mechanisms are deployed on both network and endpoint devices to protect IT infrastructure and information.

Different software, tools, and security devices are needed to protect corporate networks from ransomware attacks. There is no single solution to stop these attacks, but using the right security software and network security appliances and enforcing security policy rules will certainly lower this risk.

Installing security solutions on endpoints and using various security devices at the network perimeter are not enough to defend against ransomware attacks. An end user's cybersecurity awareness training plays a crucial role in determining whether a particular ransomware attack will succeed, and this what I cover in the next chapter.

CHAPTER 6

Security Awareness Training

Best Practices for Implementing a Security Awareness Training Program

Cybersecurity has become a major topic of discussion these days. Almost every day a new cyberattack on a corporation, government, or other entity is in the news because it resulted in millions of customer records being exposed, stolen credentials, and ransomware attacks. Cybercriminals have become increasingly sophisticated, and cybersecurity threats have escalated rapidly in recent years. Business organizations and government agencies have realized the importance of educating their employees about cybersecurity threats to safeguard against them.

All security studies related to ransomware infection and other data breaches conclude that human error is still and will continue to be the biggest threat to cybersecurity. Having a cybersecurity awareness program in your organization is vital to surviving in today's digital age and is considered the best way to prevent ransomware attacks and other threats emanating from around the globe.

A good cybersecurity awareness program will educate employees about the different cyber threats they may face when using an organization's IT system and how to mitigate and respond to these threats. All employees should know what entry points attackers can use to access their enterprise network and what precaution steps they should follow to prevent unauthorized access to information assets. The security awareness program should also enforce the security policy rules of an organization and clarify the IT security responsibility of each employee according to their job role in protecting organization information assets and IT systems.

155

© Nihad A. Hassan 2019
N. A. Hassan, *Ransomware Revealed*, https://doi.org/10.1007/978-1-4842-4255-1_6

In this chapter, I discuss the importance of having security awareness training in any organization, what topics should be included in such a training program, and how to mitigate the most common threats against computerized systems that exploit human errors, in other words, social engineering (SE) attacks.

Importance of Security Awareness Training

Every person in any organization who has access to its IT system or has an e-mail account must receive adequate cybersecurity training. Such training is important in protecting your organization from malicious actors trying to gain unauthorized access to your information assets. The following are the main benefits of conducting security awareness training in your organization.

Reduces Data Breaches and Attacks

A report published by Ponemon Institute and sponsored by Keeper Security found that negligent employees are the number-one greatest weakness when it comes to cyber threats (especially when it comes to ransomware) to small and medium-sized businesses (SMBs) across North America and the United Kingdom.[1]

Educating employees about the dangers of opening e-mail attachments from unknown sources and of clicking suspicious links in spam e-mails will greatly reduce the number of data breaches that most organizations suffer from.

Note!   A data breach is any security incident that leads to exposing personal identifying information (PII) of individuals to an outside party. PII includes the following, and more:

- Social Security numbers

- Credit card numbers

- Financial accounts

---

[1]Keepersecurity, "2017 State of Cybersecurity in Small & Medium-Sized Businesses (SMB)" October 22, 2019 https://keepersecurity.com/assets/pdf/Keeper-2017-Ponemon-Report.pdf

- Protected health information

- Usernames/passwords

- Driver license numbers

The Identity Theft Resources Center (`https://www.idtheftcenter.org/data-breaches`) maintains an updated list of data breaches worldwide since 2005.

Meets Compliance Requirements

Security awareness training becomes mandatory in many industries to comply with government laws or with other nonofficial compliance bodies working to promote information security best practices in their specific industry. For example, the Health Insurance Portability and Accountability Act (HIPAA) mandates that all organizations working in the healthcare sector (including doctors' offices) implement a security awareness training program for all staff members to protect patient information. The Payment Card Industry Data Security Standard (PCI-DSS) also imposes specialized security awareness training for all staff working in financial companies that store and process customer financial information.

> **Note!**   There are thousands of local, state, and federal standards that your organization needs to comply with. The most common rules that require an organization to have a security awareness program can be found at `https://www.knowbe4.com/resources/security-awareness-compliance-requirements/`.

Enhances Overall Organization Security and Increases Its Reputation

When employees become aware of the different cyberattack vectors and how to avoid them, their organization will become less exposed to cyber threats and data breaches, and this will consequently raise its reputation and make customers more willing to deal with it because they know their personal records are stored in safe hands.

Increases the Effectiveness of Technological Defenses

Having firewalls, intrusion prevention systems (IPSs), antivirus software, anti-malware programs, and other security solutions is great to protect against malware attacks; however, without the required IT security skills, employees cannot benefit from these solutions. For example, your firewall solution can send notifications about suspicious activity, and your OS may ask you to install required security updates. If such warnings are handled incorrectly or ignored by the end user, the technological solutions will not do their jobs correctly.

Avoids Losses from Security Incidents

A successful ransomware attack can cost an affected organization a considerable amount of time and money to recover and restore its normal operations. Obviously, without even paying the ransom, a victim company can lose a huge sum of money and hurt its reputation because of the business disruption.

Increases Employee Satisfaction

In today's digital age, employees are willing to acquire the necessary cybersecurity skills to enhance their career and to feel confident at work in addition to securing their personal digital privacy outside work. Conducting security awareness training will increase employee satisfaction, making them more willing to remain with their current company.

Best Practices When Developing a Cybersecurity Awareness Program

Having a security awareness training program will demonstrate that your organization is taking its security seriously. Aside from being required by many compliance bodies, a security awareness training program becomes the most important defense line of a defense-in-depth strategy to secure an organization's data against both internal and external attacks.

There are many areas you need to consider when developing a security awareness training program for your organization. For instance, developing a security program to comply with the PCI-DSS standard is somewhat different from one implemented to comply with HIPAA, although both aim to protect consumer data, whether it is health or financial records. In this chapter, I will not focus on the requirements of a security awareness program for a specific compliance rule. Instead, the focus will be on listing the main components of a general security awareness training program that can be implemented in any organization using IT systems.

Create the Security Awareness Team

The security awareness training program is an ongoing endeavor that requires continual monitoring and updates. The first step to creating such a training program within your organization is to establish a leadership team responsible for developing, monitoring, and implementing the security awareness training program. This team should be gathered from different departments and include staff with varying IT backgrounds (from novice to professional) to assure that your security awareness training program covers all staff levels and meet their demands.

Determine Roles for Security Awareness

A security awareness training program should teach all employees, from CEO to IT personnel, about IT security and best practices to protect information assets. However, not all staff have the same level of IT knowledge or experience. For example, the security training for an IT network engineer is different from someone in the marketing department who uses their computer to access the corporate customer relationship management (CRM) database.

Your security awareness training materials should be tailored according to each employee level of responsibility and their job role in the organization. For example, you can divide employees within an organization into four major groups based on their job roles and associate each group with the appropriate security awareness training.

- **Executive level (CEO)**: People at this level (high-profile employees or the C level) are usually not tech-savvy. The major cyber threat against them is social engineering attacks (especially spear phishing and whaling). Training at this level should be focused around mitigating social engineering attacks with easy-to-understand examples.

- **IT department**: Training for the IT staff should be more technical and focused on how to mitigate and respond to cyber incidents. Some digital forensics materials should be incorporated into this level, as those people should know how to behave if a data breach or ransomware attack takes place.

- **Management staff**: At this level, general security awareness training is required to teach the fundamentals of IT security and best practices to avoid data breaches. The management staff has also another role, which is enforcing implementing security policy rules in addition to what they learn from security awareness training on other employees.

- **All staff**: Training materials should be tailored according to their general job role, mainly mitigating phishing e-mails and following security policy when using their computing devices to access the corporate network, checking e-mails, or plugging USB devices into work machines.

Note!   Tailoring your security awareness training program materials according to the employee's job role within an organization will save your employees training time and reduce training costs for your organization.

Topics Covered in Cybersecurity Awareness Training

The security awareness training program can be delivered in various ways such as e-learning (online), formal training, e-mail, bulletins, written guides, and other means. The materials should cover all aspects of cybersecurity relevant to each user's job role to have the most intensive impact on employees.

The following are the main topics that should be covered during a security awareness training program:

- **Introduction to cybersecurity**: Introduce information security and why it is important for both individuals and enterprises. Identify current threats and different attack vectors. Explain the challenges of securing IT systems.

- **Personal security**: Personal security is concerned with educating end users about best practices to secure their personal accounts and endpoint devices. Topics in this section include: password selection criteria, utilizing passwords safely during storage and usage, attacks against encryption systems (acquiring your password/key illegally), social engineering attacks and how to mitigate them, personal cybersecurity defense, and risks associated with using social media web sites (e.g., revealing sensitive information about work and personal life that could be exploited by attackers).

- **Computer security**: In this section, a user should learn how to differentiate between different types of malware and how each type can be introduced to the system; about the importance of using various security solutions (e.g., antivirus, anti-malware, firewall) to protect endpoint devices, network, and other entry points; and about the importance of creating backups of data and securing data assets and OS using encryption techniques. Cloud security also should be introduced in this section.

- **Internet security**: This topic should include e-mail and web browser security risks and how to avoid them, installing security add-ons for your web browser to mitigate some online risks (e.g., block malvertising and pop-up ads), using different services to reveal malicious web sites, using a VPN to secure your online traffic, and understanding how attackers can exploit web browser vulnerabilities to gain unauthorized access and anything related to Internet safety.

- **Mobile security**: In this section, an employee should understand how intruders can exploit WiFi networks to gain unauthorized access, learn about the risks associated with using mobile technology and the Internet of Things (IoT) devices, understand the security policy of an organization regarding using personal mobile devices at work, learn how to secure your mobile device, and learn how to use the public WiFi network securely.

- **Enforcing security policy rules**: In the previous chapter, I already covered the importance of having a security policy in place to govern the usage/access of an organization's IT assets and resources. Security awareness training should focus on educating employees on how to implement the security policy rules and clarify any vague points if they do not know how to implement the rules in reality.

Official Reference Materials to Develop a Security Awareness Training Program

There are many government organizations and industry bodies that promote the development of the security awareness training program and suggest training materials. The following are the most popular ones:

- National Institute of Standards and Technology's Special Publication 800-50, "Building an Information Technology Security Awareness and Training Program" (`https://csrc.nist.gov/publications/detail/sp/800-50/final`)

- ISO/IEC 27002:2013, "Information technology – Security techniques – Code of practice for information security controls" (`https://www.iso.org/standard/54533.html`)

- COBIT 5 Framework (`http://www.isaca.org/cobit/pages/default.aspx`)

Security Awareness Training Content

We already covered the main topics that should be included in any security awareness training program. Most of these topics have been covered in the previous chapters. However, as you have learned throughout the book, the most common techniques to infect with ransomware are malicious e-mails (phishing e-mail) and other social engineering attacks. For this reason, the rest of this chapter covers in some detail how to recognize and prevent social engineering attacks, especially phishing, which is considered the starting point for most network and data breaches.

Social Engineering Attacks

Social engineering, in the context of information security, is a kind of cybersecurity attack that uses psychological tricks over the phone, through direct contact, or in e-mail messages to convince unaware users to reveal confidential information about themselves (e.g., social account credentials, financial information, or credit card details) or about the enterprise where they work (e.g., type of IT infrastructure, entry points to organization network, type of security defenses in place). Many SE attacks aim to deceive a victim into installing malicious software on their PC to gain full control over the targeted machine and to use it to spread the infection to other places within the network.

Malicious actors use SE tactics that are based on exploiting human errors rather than exploiting system and software vulnerabilities to gain unauthorized access or to infect with malware. Obviously, this makes predicting such attacks hard as no one can predict the human behaviors in such cases.

There are two main types of SE attacks in term of the medium used to launch the attack. The first one relies on e-mail messages and is more common, and the second uses phone and in-person tricks. Please note an attacker can use both types to gain useful insight about the target before launching an attack.

E-mail Phishing Attacks

A phishing e-mail is a type of SE attack that uses an e-mail message, the instant messaging feature of social media services and apps (e.g., Facebook), or a text message (SMS) to acquire sensitive information from a victim or to install malware (e.g., ransomware) through e-mail attachments and malicious links on their machine. Such attacks can have devastating consequences on both personal and enterprise security. For example, an individual's confidential information can be acquired through impersonating a trusted entity (e.g., legitimate bank, government agency, or social networking service) to lure the victim into disclosing sensitive information (usually by clicking a link in the malicious e-mail that takes the victim to a fake web page to enter/update personal data). Once this information is obtained, an attacker can use it to blackmail the victim, make unauthorized purchases using stolen credentials, or use such information (e.g., employee login credentials) to launch an advanced attack against a target company. Attackers can also use the same phishing e-mails to install a keylogger on victim machines to steal sensitive information silently. In an enterprise context, the losses can be greater. For instance, most advanced persistent threat (APT) attacks use phishing e-mails as an entry point to surpass all network security perimeters to infect and propagate ransomware in a closed environment or to gain unauthorized access to secure areas within the target enterprise network.

Therefore, phishing awareness training is an essential component in any security awareness training program. Phishing is still the number-one attack vector and is considered the main concern for IT security professionals when working to implement a defense-in-depth (DiD) strategy. To understand how to spot phishing e-mails, you need to know what they look like.

Note!   According to the "Phishing Activity Trends" report published by APWG, more than 90,000 unique phishing campaigns are launched every month.[2]

What Does a Phishing E-mail Message Look Like?

In this section, we will look at a sample phishing e-mail (see Figure 6-1) to investigate its different components and see how its contents differ from other legitimate e-mails.

[2]APWG, "Phishing Activity Trends Report" May 29, 2019 https://docs.apwg.org/reports/ apwg_trends_report_h1_2017.pdf

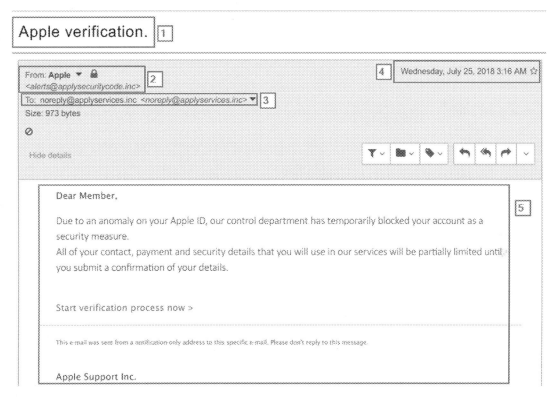

Figure 6-1. *Sample phishing e-mail showing different parts of each e-mail message, described next*

1: E-mail subject line

- Check the e-mail subject line. Phishing e-mails commonly use urgent, threatening, or scary words in the subject line to convince the recipient to act promptly without thinking. For example, in Figure 6-2, we have a phishing e-mail with a threatening subject. According to Barracuda Networks' "Spear Phishing: Top Threats and Trends"[3] report, the most used e-mail phishing subjects are the following: Request, Follow up, Urgent/Important, Are you available?/Are you at your desk?, Payment Status, Hello, Purchase, Invoice Due, Re:, Direct Deposit, Expenses, and Payroll.

---

[3]Barracuda, "Spear Phishing: Top Threats and Trends" May 29, 2019 https://www.barracuda.com/spear-phishing-report

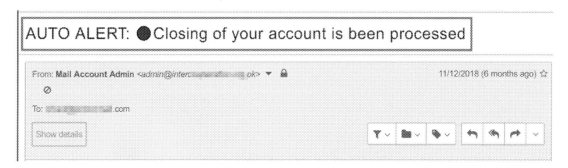

Figure 6-2. *Sample e-mail with the threatening subject of account closure*

2: E-mail "From" field

- The subject e-mail pretends to be from the Apple Corporation; however, the sender e-mail does not originate from the Apple domain name (apple.com). Instead, it is from applysecuritycode.inc.

  Keep in mind that the domain name in the "From" field does not need to be authentic, as attackers can spoof other legitimate domain names to mislead unaware users.

- Now, you need to ask yourself the following questions regarding the sender e-mail address:

  a. Do you know the sender? If yes, do you trust him?

  b. Does the sender's e-mail address match up with the sender name (e.g., nihad.hassan@darknessgate.com and a sender name of Nihad Hassan)?

  c. Do you have any business relationship with the sender or with this company?

  d. Read the sender e-mail address carefully, and check any misspellings in the sender domain name. For example, marketing@darknessgate.com can be misspelled to become marketing@darknessgate.info (a different domain extension) or marketing@darknesssgate.com (an additional "s").

e. Investigate the sender domain name to see whether it is listed
    as malicious. There are many free services to check whether
    a particular domain name is malicious, as covered in the
    previous chapter. However, the following are additional web
    sites for looking up potentially malicious and phishing web
    sites:

    i.   Norton Safe Web (`https://safeweb.norton.com`)

    ii. IsItPhishing (`https://isitphishing.org`)

    iii. Phishtank (`https://www.phishtank.com`)

    iv. Virus Total (`https://www.virustotal.com/#/home/url`)

    v.   AbuseIPDB (`https://www.abuseipdb.com`)

    vi. Kaspersky VirusDesk (`https://virusdesk.kaspersky.com`)

f. Did you initiate this conversation? For example, if someone
    sends you an e-mail asking for your personal information
    because you won the lottery, ask yourself the following
    question: Did you participate in that lottery and ask to receive
    such e-mails?

- If you have a business relationship with the sender, then move on
  and read the e-mail content carefully. Does it ask you to reveal your
  account credentials? Or to download an attachment that seems
  suspicious (e.g., a zipped file or Microsoft Office or PDF file)? In such
  a case, try to communicate directly with the sender via phone or
  indirectly to remove any doubt.

3: The "To" field

- From Figure 6-1, you can note that the e-mail is sent to noreply@
  applyservices.inc. This means the e-mail was sent to many users
  at once and is not directed solely to the intended recipient. Such
  e-mails can be a part of a large spam campaign.

- If the e-mail "CC" field is populated with addresses, check them one
  by one. Do you know any of them? Is the domain name of any e-mail
  in the "CC" field is blacklisted and marked as malicious?

4: E-mail date/time sent

- Check the e-mail sent time. If the e-mail pretends to be from your company or bank, did they send it during official work hours? Check the date also, did they send it during holidays? In (Figure 6-1) the e-mail sent time was 3:16 a.m. Obviously, no one would send e-mails at that time!

Note!   You can check the time zone of any place on earth by going to `https://www.timeanddate.com/time/map/`. You can also check holidays and observances around the world via the same web site by going to `https://www.timeanddate.com/holidays/`.

5: Investigate e-mail content (body), URLs, and any attachments

- Hover your mouse over the hyperlink in the e-mail body to reveal the true address; for this example, it points to another domain (`https://tinyurl.com/yde7qbvd`) other than the one it pretends to be from (Apple.com).

- Spammers tend to use a URL shortening service such as Bitly (`https://bitly.com`), TinyURL (`https://tinyurl.com`), or Tinycc (`https://tiny.cc`) to mask their malicious hyperlinks. If you encounter such a situation, you can expand any shortened URL using a free URL expander service (see Figure 6-3) such as checkshorturl (`https://checkshorturl.com`), expandURL (`https://www.expandurl.net`), urlxray (`http://urlxray.com`), or URLEX (`https://urlex.org`). In Figure 6-1, the "Start verification process now" link goes to the following URL: `https://tinyurl.com/yde7qbvd`. To reveal the true address, go to any of the previously mentioned URL expander services to unshorten it (see Figure 6-3).

Figure 6-3. *Using* `https://urlex.org` *to find the true masked address of a shortened URL*

- If you receive an e-mail without any content that contains only a hyperlink inside it, make sure not to click this link and investigate it as explained.

- Read the e-mail body carefully. Does the sender mention your name or simply use a generic salutation such as "Dear Member" or "Dear Valued customer"? Using a generic greeting is common in spam campaigns because the messages are sent in bulk and do not address a specific person.

Warning!   In spear phishing and whaling (which is a personalized phishing e-mail attack), an attacker collects different personal information about the target using open source intelligence (OSINT) techniques before targeting them with a phishing e-mail. In this case, the e-mail will be crafted well using the victim's first and last names.

- Phishing e-mails commonly contain grammatical errors and are poorly written. When you see a poorly written e-mail that pretends to be from a government agency or financial institution such as your bank, then this is likely to be a phishing e-mail.

- Does the sender ask you to provide your personal information? Or to verify your account details? Or even to send your password to avoid account closure? Legitimate companies do not send e-mails asking about your personal information or your account credentials because they already have this information.

- Does the e-mail contain strange attachments? For example, if you receive an e-mail with an executable attachment, then this should raise a red flag because legitimate organizations do not send executables via e-mail messages, even for their employees. Instead, they upload such files to the cloud and send a link to the intended user to download it.

- Is it common for the sender to send you e-mail with attachments? Or to send files via social media services such as Facebook? If not, then it is safer to not open such files before verifying them with the sender. As you already saw, ransomware can disguise itself in Microsoft Office macros, PDFs, compressed files such as ZIP and 7z, and some types of image files. Such file types are common in the business world, and you should be cautious when receiving such file types via e-mail attachments.

- Business e-mails usually contain full business addresses, including a phone number, in the sender e-mail signature. If you suspect the signature contains false information, make sure to visit the company web site to verify the information. You should also avoid clicking social media links included in the e-mail signature unless you trust the sender.

Countermeasures Against Phishing Attacks

E-mail phishing attacks can be mitigated using a combination of security tools and end-user training. The following are the key issues to consider:

- Educate your employees about phishing attacks so all staff members can recognize phishing e-mails and understand the security risks associated with such e-mails.

- Do not send any personal or sensitive work information via e-mail systems. Even though you know a sender is legitimate, the sender may not have the necessary security tools in place to protect their end (e.g., opening your e-mail over the insecure HTTP connection), which may result in revealing e-mail content to outside attackers.

- When you are in doubt, do not click any link contained in the received e-mail and investigate the links as mentioned. If you receive an e-mail from your bank regarding updating your account information, make sure to access your bank account portal by typing the address directly in the browser address bar, and avoid clicking the provided link within the received e-mail.

- Make sure all the traffic with your webmail is conducted over a secure connection (SSL certificate).

- Do not access your e-mail account using free, open WiFi access points in public places. If you are in a situation where you need to use such free Internet access, make sure to use a reliable VPN service first.

- Do not reply to spam e-mails. Delete them permanently.

- Be extremely cautious about e-mail attachments and do not open attachments from unknown senders. If you need to open a file or execute a program sent via e-mail, make sure to open/run them inside a virtual machine such as VirtualBox (`https://www.virtualbox.org/wiki/Downloads`).

- Use the phone to talk with the sender to confirm any suspicious e-mail.

- Disable HTML in your e-mail system to prevent executing any code in the received e-mails.

- Consider encrypting your e-mails when exchanging confidential information.

- Do not enter any information or react to pop-up windows when browsing online. Reputable web sites do not use such a method to interact with their visitors.

- Do not publish your primary e-mail online, as mentioned in the previous chapter. If a company wants to publish its employees' work e-mail on its web site, then it should do this in a way that prevents e-mail bots from collecting them automatically.

- Makes sure your endpoint device OS is up-to-date along with your installed security solutions such as antivirus, antispam, and anti-malware.

- Use two-factor authentication when possible to prevent attackers from gaining unauthorized access to critical business applications.

- Use a strong password to protect your e-mail account; consider my tips for creating secure passwords in Chapter 5.

- Do not use a free e-mail service for mission-critical tasks. Free e-mail providers monitor users' e-mail to target them with customized advertisements.

- Do not reveal information about the company you work for. Attackers can use such information to customize their phishing attacks (spear and whaling phishing).

Phone-Based and In-Person Attacks

E-mail phishing is the preferred method to acquire sensitive information or to install malicious software on unaware users' computers. However, there are other social engineering techniques to exploit human errors such as the following:

- **Shoulder surfing**: This means acquiring user passwords by watching them type them on the keyboard.

- **Dumpster diving**: This means acquiring confidential information from materials thrown in the trash (e.g., papers, CDs/DVDs, and data on faulty hard drives and other portable media devices disposed of insecurely in the trash).

- **Role-playing**: In this kind of attack, an attacker will impersonate technical support staff at some company and try to get sensitive information from users to gain illegal access to their accounts.

- **OSINT**: Open source intelligence (OSINT) is where attackers investigate publicly published information about a specific entity (company or individual) to gain intelligence. Different tools exist to perform these attacks; you can find many of them at `www.OSINT.link`.

Note!   To learn more about exploiting OSINT sources to gather intelligence, please refer to my OSINT book titled *Open Source Intelligence Methods and Tools* (Apress, 2018).

As mentioned, there are different types of social engineering attacks, and all try to exploit the "human error factor," which remains the weakest element in computer security, to gain unauthorized access or to install malware on target machines. End-user cybersecurity awareness training is considered the best countermeasure against such attacks.

Summary

Employees are still the most important assets in your organization. Failing to educate them on how to identify and respond to security threats can have a devastating impact on your organization's work and reputation. Therefore, it is essential for any organization utilizing IT technology to have security awareness training in place that incorporates the essential guidelines to prevent and counter cyber incidents.

Developing a security awareness training program will incur costs; however, when comparing this cost with the possible losses as a result of a successful penetration into your organization's IT system that may lead to a data breach or a ransomware infection, then it will for sure pay off the price.

In computer security, there is no 100 percent foolproof solution. If you follow all the preventive measures in this part of the book and you fall victim to a ransomware attack, then the next part of this book will tell you how to respond and recover from such an incident.

PART III

Dealing with Ransomware Incidents

CHAPTER 7

Paying the Ransom

Should You Pay?

Regardless of all mitigation measures or prevention strategies already described in this book, no organization or individual can be 100 percent immune to ransomware infection. This makes having a solid backup and recovery plan important to counter successful ransomware attacks.

So, the most important question is, what should you do if you do not have the appropriate backup to restore operations after a ransomware infection? Let's imagine a scenario where ransomware infects the victim's backup data also. What you can do in such a situation?

In such a horrible situation, you are limited to one of these options:

- Remove the infection and try to decrypt the infected data.

- Do nothing. Wipe the infected machine's software and install a clean OS and applications.

- Pay the ransom.

The first option, removing the ransomware infection using special decryption tools, will be the subject of the next chapter; however, this option depends on the existence of a decryption utility for the specific ransomware. The second option is to do nothing; in this scenario, you lose all your infected data and start from zero. The third option, which is paying the ransom, is the subject of this chapter.

In this chapter, I show how to evaluate whether to pay a ransom. This is a tough question because it largely depends on each case. I also talk about the anonymous payment methods employed by ransomware owners when receiving money from their victims. Obviously, having a secure, anonymous payment system in place that cannot be traced is a key element in the ransomware attack model.

© Nihad A. Hassan 2019
N. A. Hassan, *Ransomware Revealed*, https://doi.org/10.1007/978-1-4842-4255-1_7

Choosing to Pay the Ransom

My advice to you is to *never* pay a ransom to unlock your locked files! Remember, you are dealing with criminals, and those people lack the ethics to respect their commitments. Besides, paying money to cybercriminals will encourage them to intensify their attacks and invest part of the ransom money into developing more devastating code to evade detection and to target more people in the future.

On the other hand, the risk of data loss in today's information age can have catastrophic consequences on a victim's enterprise. A successful ransomware attack could even put the target enterprise out of business, with all the damage to its reputation and bottom line; in some cases it could even cost lives if ransomware hits healthcare organizations and denies access to critical patient records.

Note!   Some enterprises prefer to pay the ransom to restore their services as quickly as possible to limit downtime, despite having the necessary backups to restore their normal operations.

Ransomware creators generally request low ransoms from individual victims, usually between $300 to $2,000 USD. Some ransomware variants request more (about $286,000 as with the Ryuk ransomware and up to $600,000 as with the case of Riviera Beach City, Florida[1]), especially in tailored attacks against high-value targets when hundreds of machines, storage, and data centers are infected.

Paying a ransom can be considered a cost-effective solution to the problem. For example, the recovery costs from the SamSam ransomware that hit the City of Atlanta in March 2018 may exceed $17 million, according to a report obtained by the *Atlanta Journal-Constitution* and Channel 2 Action News.[2] This number is huge compared with the ransom payment, which was worth $50,000 Bitcoin at that time.

---

[1]Securityaffairs, "The Riviera Beach City pays $600,000 in ransom" June 26, 2019 `https://securityaffairs.co/wordpress/87381/breaking-news/riviera-beach-city-ransomware.html`

[2]AJC, "CONFIDENTIAL REPORT: Atlanta's cyber-attack could cost taxpayers $17 million" June 15, 2019 `https://www.ajc.com/news/confidential-report-atlanta-cyber-attack-could-hit-million/GAljmndAF3EQdVWlMcXSOK/?icmp=np_inform_variation-control`

Keeping all these things in mind, a victim can weigh the possibilities and select the best option that reflects the current conditions. Paying a ransom can be the only feasible solution to restore locked data in many cases. In this section, I discuss the different payment methods used by ransomware authors to receive ransoms from their victims.

Anonymous Payments

Ransomware owners use different anonymous payment methods to receive their funds. The most popular and risk-free method is cryptocurrency, covered next.

Cryptocurrency

This type of digital cash system is designed to work as a medium of exchange using cryptographic protocols to secure the transaction and to control the creation of additional units of currency. There is no central authority—or main server—that governs the usage and creation of cryptocurrency. People can use cryptocurrency to buy products and services in addition to exchanging it privately and anonymously without revealing their true identity.

Bitcoin was the first decentralized cryptocurrency, appearing in 2009, and remains the dominant currency in terms of use and capitalization. It is also considered the preferred payment method for criminals to receive their ransoms funds, so it will be the focus of this section.

Bitcoin

Bitcoin remains the most popular cryptocurrency for ransomware payments. According to "Coveware,[3]" 98 percent of ransomware attacks request payment via Bitcoin.

Bitcoin (`https://bitcoin.org`) is an innovative open source Internet protocol that uses an SHA-256 cryptographic hash. It was created by a Japanese software developer named Satoshi Nakamoto. Bitcoin is a decentralized peer-to-peer payment network (similar to file sharing networks such as Torrent) that is powered by its users with no central authority (e.g., government central bank) or middleman. Bitcoin is a digital cash system; it is not printed like ordinary currency and is created by people and corporations

---

[3]Coveware, "Ransom amounts rise 90% in Q1 as Ryuk increases," June 13, 2019
`https://www.coveware.com/blog/2019/4/15/ransom-amounts-rise-90-in-q1-as-ryuk-ransomware-increases`

using a specific mining mechanism.[4] Bitcoin is received, stored, and sent using a specialized software program called a Bitcoin wallet (the wallet can be an online service, called an *e-wallet*). Bitcoin does not charge fees on transactions, and it is nonrefundable. (Once you send Bitcoins to a recipient, it will be gone forever you're your account, unless the recipient returns them to you.)

Tip!   There are hundreds of cryptocurrency types already in use. CoinMarketCap (`https://coinmarketcap.com`) lists most of them. In addition to Bitcoin, Dash and Monero are used by a few ransomware strains to receive ransom funds.

To pay via Bitcoin, you must have a Bitcoin account filled with Bitcoin currency, covered next.

Open a Bitcoin Account

Like with a traditional bank account, you need a Bitcoin account number to send or receive funds to or from it. In Bitcoin terms, this called an *address*. A Bitcoin address is a single-use token that looks like this: 14r9k2Rq2PZhGRc7dsi2j1KQ7fJEZwbcVe.

There is no limit on the number of Bitcoin addresses each user can have, and all these addresses are stored in a user's Bitcoin wallet.

A Bitcoin wallet is a software program that can be installed on your computer or smartphone as an app; the wallet is used to create a Bitcoin address, send and receive Bitcoin, and keep track of your Bitcoin transaction history. You can download the official Bitcoin wallet program from `https://wallet.bitcoin.com`.

In addition, many online services offer a Bitcoin wallet service for investing and storing cryptocurrencies. At `https://www.blockchain.com/wallet`, you can sign up for a new Bitcoin wallet by entering a valid e-mail and password (this password is to access your Bitcoin wallet). To see your Bitcoin address, log in to your wallet account and click the Request button (see Figure 7-1).

---

[4]Buybitcoinworldwide, "What is Bitcoin Mining and How Does it Work?" June 15, 2019 `https://www.buybitcoinworldwide.com/mining/`

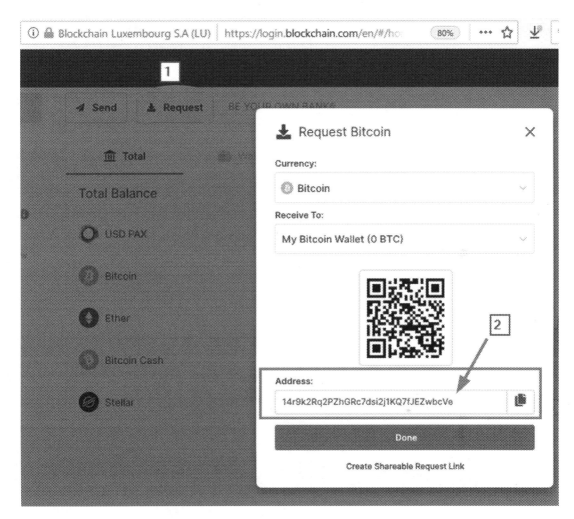

Figure 7-1. *Viewing the Bitcoin account address at* www.blockchain.com

---

Warning!   If you are planning to store some money in your Bitcoin wallet, then it is advisable to use a software-based Bitcoin wallet instead of the online wallet services, which have suffered from many security breaches in the past. To see a list of available Bitcoin wallets (desktop, mobile, hardware), go to https://bitcoin.org/en/choose-your-wallet.

Buy Bitcoin

Now that you have a Bitcoin account, you need to fuel it with cash to pay for goods and services—and possibly ransoms!—in Bitcoin. Keep in mind that Bitcoin is a form of currency, so to use it, you need to buy it first using traditional money (e.g., U.S. dollars or euros). In this section, I list different methods to fund your newly created Bitcoin wallet with cash.

If you are following along and have created your wallet at Blockchain.com, you can get Bitcoin currency by logging into your Bitcoin wallet and then clicking the Buy & Sell option on the left side of the page (see Figure 7-2). Currently, Blockchain.com works with exchange partners all around the world; select your country from the drop-down menu and click the Next button to continue (see Figure 7-2).

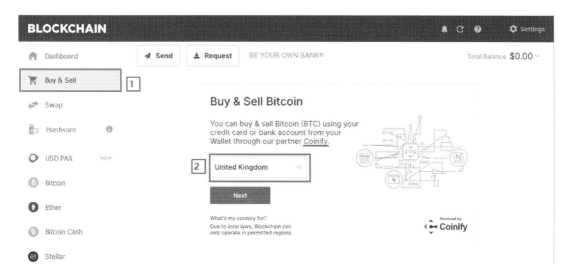

Figure 7-2. *Selecting the country where you reside to see available partners to buy and sell Bitcoin*

The next window will create an account for you on the Bitcoin exchange partner that you select in the first step; fill in your personal and mail address and then click Continue to proceed. In the next window, you need to enter a valid government ID to authenticate your details with the partner exchange company. Follow the steps to get verified.

After verifying your identity, you can specify the amount of Bitcoin you want to purchase from the Buy & Sell button, pay using either a bank transfer or a credit/debit card, and store them in your Bitcoin wallet.

Alternative Anonymous Methods to Buy Bitcoin

Obviously, when using the previous method to buy Bitcoin, you will reveal your true identity as you are using your bank account or credit/debit card to purchase Bitcoin. Nevertheless, if you want to buy Bitcoin anonymously, here are some alternative, anonymous methods:

- **Cash**: This is the best anonymous option. Find someone to sell you their Bitcoin in person. You can find potential sellers by going to `https://localbitcoins.com` and arranging an in-person meeting to buy or sell Bitcoins. To use this service, you need to open an account, which requires only an e-mail and password. To remain anonymous, make sure not to use your primary e-mail address; instead, use an e-mail address that is not tied to your real identity.

- **ATM machines**: You can buy Bitcoin anonymously with cash using Bitcoin ATM machines; there are approximately 1,400+ ATMs worldwide, but these machines are not available everywhere. Bitcoin ATM machines allow you to generate a new Bitcoin address if you do not supply one, and this new address will be printed on paper. Then you can take this paper and import the private keys on it to your e-wallet online service or Bitcoin client software. To find ATM machines that support Bitcoin, go to `https://coinatmradar.com`. From here you can select your country/city and see a list of ATMs along with their physical locations; you can buy the Bitcoin from these machines using cash.

- **Prepaid cards**: This type of anonymous payment will be covered in the next section; you can use such cards (usually found in shopping centers) to buy Bitcoin online without providing any personal details. However, to remain anonymous, make sure to use anonymize your connection using the TOR network and a secondary e-mail address to conduct the buying transaction. The sites `https://www.coinmama.com` and `https://paxful.com` accept gift cards to buy Bitcoin.

Note!   It is not advisable to store a large sum of money in your Bitcoin wallet, even though you are using the software wallet version, as the Bitcoin price has a high fluctuation rate compared with traditional currencies. You can always buy Bitcoin using any of the methods already described to fund your wallet when you need to use it.

Make Payments

After you have currency in your Bitcoin address, you are ready to make online purchases or send payments to other Bitcoin accounts. To do so, follow these steps:

1. Find the Bitcoin account address that you want to send money to.

2. Go to the web site you used to get your address from (in my case `https://blockchain.com`). Access your wallet dashboard and click the Send button (see Figure 7-3).

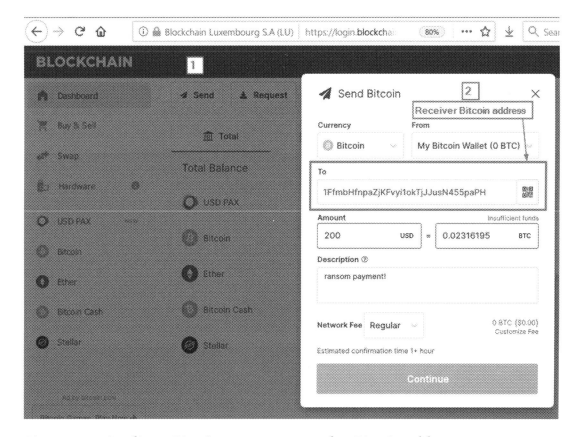

Figure 7-3. *Sending a Bitcoin payment to another Bitcoin address*

3. Find the location where you input your recipient's address, specify the amount of money you want to send, and finally click Continue to proceed.

This is how you use Bitcoin to make online payments and send transactions; as noted, it is straightforward.

Warning!   Encrypt your online connection (e.g., using a VPN service) before making an anonymous payment.

How a Typical Ransomware Payment Transaction Works

The following steps demonstrate how a ransom transaction works (see Figure 7-4):

1. After infecting a victim computer with ransomware, a ransom note appears on the screen with detailed instructions on how to pay the ransom (attackers usually provide instructions on how to open a Bitcoin account and purchase Bitcoin).

2. The victim purchases Bitcoin and adds them to their Bitcoin wallet.

3. The victim sends the required ransom amount to the attacker's Bitcoin address, which can be found in the ransom note.

4. The criminal confirms receiving the ransom, and if everything goes well, the criminal will send the decryption key via e-mail or via the criminal's TOR web site so that the victim can decrypt their files.

5. Criminals usually launder the received Bitcoins using a Bitcoin mixer service (also known as *Bitcoin tumbling*). This process helps criminals conceal their identity by using a third-party service that scrambles the connection between the sender and received Bitcoin addresses to avoid being caught by law enforcement. Popular Bitcoin tumbling services include BitMix.Biz (`https://bitmix.biz/en`), Bitcoin Blender (`https://bitblender.io`), and mixtum (`https://mixtum.io`).

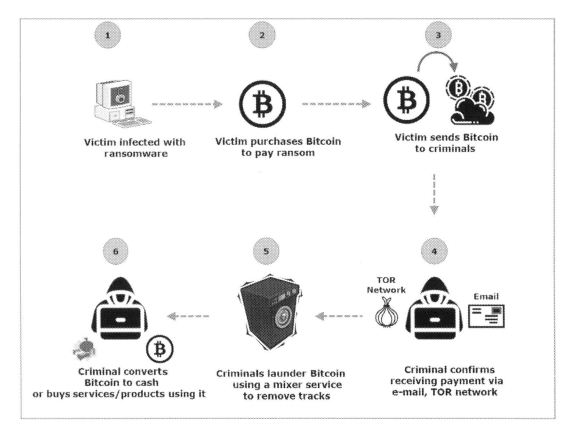

Figure 7-4. *Ransom transaction using Bitcoin cryptocurrency*

Prepaid Gift Cards

Another method to pay ransomware operators is via prepaid payment methods. For instance, old ransomware strains demanded money via a premium rate SMS message and the old defunct Ukash vouchers (now called *paysafecard*).

It is rare for modern ransomware strains to request payments via prepaid gift cards. Despite this, some unpopular variants are still using such method. For example, the Alpha ransomware demands its payments via an iTunes gift card, while TrueCrypter ransomware requests its payment in Amazon gift cards.

Most credit card providers offer prepaid cards for their clients. This type of card can be used just like an ordinary one, and it does not require a client to have a credit check or bank account. In addition, most prepaid cards don't require a PIN to use.

There are different types of prepaid gifts cards. What we care about for this discussion is the anonymous type, which is the "nonreloadable" card. Prepaid cards (the nonreloadable type) are available almost everywhere, from drug stores to supermarkets. You can purchase them with cash (untraceable) without providing any personal information or contact information.

As mentioned, Bitcoin will remain the preferred risk-free payment method for criminals to collect their ransoms in the foreseeable future.

What Should I Do If I've Already Paid?

The first thing you need to do is to report the incident to authorities. This will help security companies and independent security researchers create a decryptor for the reported ransomware. In addition, it will help authorities track criminals and prevent them from continuing their malicious activities.

Warning!   Paying ransoms can violate certain laws in your country, as ransom payments can go to funding other illegal activities (e.g., buying drugs or weapons) of criminal/terrorist organizations.

In developed countries, there is a special authority to report ransomware and other cyberattacks; however, if you are based in a country where you do not know where to report ransomware attacks, then simply go to the nearest police department to report the incident, and they will escalate the incident to the appropriate department.

The following are the main authorities in selected countries to report ransomware incidents:

- **United States**: On Guard Online (`https://www.consumer.ftc.gov/features/feature-0038-onguardonline`), FBI (`https://www.fbi.gov/contact-us/field-offices`), or Internet Crime Complaint Center (`https://www.ic3.gov/default.aspx`)

- **United Kingdom**: Action Fraud (`https://www.actionfraud.police.uk`)

- **Australia**: Scam Watch (`https://www.scamwatch.gov.au`)

- **Canada**: Anti-Fraud Centre (`http://www.antifraudcentre-centreantifraude.ca/index-eng.htm`)

- **New Zealand**: Consumer Protection (`https://www.consumerprotection.govt.nz/general-help/scamwatch`)

- **Germany**: BSI (`https://www.bsi.bund.de/DE/Home/home_node.html`)

- **Belgium**: Police (`https://www.police.be/en`)

- **Finland**: Police of Finland (`https://www.poliisi.fi/crimes/reporting_an_offence_online`)

- **France**: Internet Signalement (`https://www.internet-signalement.gouv.fr/PortailWeb/planets/Accueil!input.action`)

To report cybercrime online for other EU countries, check the Europol web site (`https://www.europol.europa.eu/report-a-crime/report-cybercrime-online`).

Choosing to Not Pay the Ransom

As mentioned, choosing to pay or not pay the ransom will depend on each case. Many enterprises will select to pay the ransom to avoid ceasing their work and consequently damaging the business. However, when you pay money to ransomware perpetrators, remember that you are dealing with the bad guys. You cannot trust their word, and there is no guarantee that you will be able to restore your files.

Ransomware authors try to convince their victims via ransom notes that their hostage files are irretrievable if they refuse to pay the ransom. This fact is not always true as security companies and other nongovernment bodies are continually developing decryption tools for each discovered ransomware strain. If your data is not critical and you can recover part of it from backup, then a wise solution is to wait until there is a decryptor for your infected data.

Many ransomware operators return to hit the same target after receiving the ransom. Besides, some criminals request more money after receiving the original payment amount to release the decryption key. On the other hand, some ransomware variants such as NotPetya will not recover your encrypted files even after you pay the ransom.

Finally, paying a ransom will fund the perpetrators behind it and result in them creating more sophisticated code to target more people with ransomware. And remember that the threat actors behind ransomware can belong to terrorist groups or oppressive regimes that may use ransom payments to fund terror attacks and other malicious activities.

Of course, when your business data is encrypted and you do not have the necessary backup to restore operations, paying the ransom will be the easiest option to get rid of the problem, so you may not care about all these other considerations! However, keep in mind that there is always a work-around solution, and you should not pay the ransom before evaluating all your available options.

Summary

Each ransomware incident is unique, so I cannot give specific advice to handle all ransomware attacks. In this chapter, you evaluated whether to pay a ransom, taking into account all possible options. If you are struck by a ransomware attack, do not panic. Seek help from specialized firms or from your experienced colleagues and report the incident to authorities. Make sure to conduct an online search to gain more information about the ransomware strain and see how other people have handled a similar attack.

It is always advisable to *not* pay the ransom even though this may result in disturbing your business; remember, there is no guarantee that ransomware operators will respect their promise and deliver the decryption key after payment. But if you decide to pay the ransom, you now know how to use Bitcoin and other anonymous payment methods to make the payment. After you pay the ransom, you must wipe clean your OS and applications after recovering your important data as ransomware operators could plant other ransomware in your system and network to launch future attacks.

In the next chapter, you will see how you can recover from ransomware incidents without paying a ransom by using available decryption tools and some work-around techniques.

CHAPTER 8

Ransomware Decryption Tools

Remove Ransomware Infection Without Paying the Ransom

As mentioned in the previous chapter, if you don't have a backup, if your computer gets infected with ransomware, you have three options to select from.

- Remove the infection with a decryptor and try to decrypt the infected data.

- Do nothing. Wipe the infected machine's software and install a clean OS and applications.

- Pay the ransom.

Paying a ransom is not a recommended option and is not guaranteed to restore your data (according to Bleepingcomputer.com, half of ransomware victims do not recover their infected data after paying the ransom demand[1]). However, a victim may not have the necessary backup to restore the infected files. This leaves one possible option to restore infected data, which is to use a third-party decryptor.

Whether you have a backup of the infected data or not, you should conduct an online search to see whether the ransomware that hit your system already has a decryptor. Sometimes restoring data from backup may disturb your work as it needs some time to complete. Using a reliable decryptor can be a more efficient solution.

---

[1]Bleepingcomputer, "Only Half of Those Who Paid a Ransomware Were Able to Recover Their Data" June 28, 2019 https://www.bleepingcomputer.com/news/security/only-half-of-those-who-paid-a-ransomware-were-able-to-recover-their-data

With the continual growing threat of ransomware attacks, security vendors are investing in creating decryptors for various ransomware families. Many security firms and independent security researchers will launch a decryptor soon after a ransomware strain appears. Although a third-party decryptor is not guaranteed to work 100 percent of the time, trying these tools will cost you nothing and may recover your data without paying a ransom. Please note that using decryption tools requires some level of technical expertise. In addition, each tool is only able to recover data infected by a specific ransomware strain; in other words, there is no one general decryptor for all ransomware types.

In this chapter, I introduce some ransomware decryptors and also explain a manual method to recover from locking ransomware. However, before you begin your search for a suitable ransomware decryptor for your problem, you need to identify the type of ransomware you have been infected with.

Identify the Ransomware You've Been Infected With

To identify the type of ransomware that has struck your system, use any of the following services:

- **ID Ransomware** (`https://id-ransomware.malwarehunterteam.com`): This is a free service that identifies the ransomware type infecting your computer. It detects more than 726 types of ransomware and advises the user if there is a decryptor or a method to decrypt the infected data. To use this service, just upload the ransom note or upload a sample encrypted file to the service, and it will determine the ransomware type for you.

- **No More Ransom** (`https://www.nomoreransom.org/crypto-sheriff.php`): This service allows you to determine the ransomware type affecting your device. To use this service, you can upload a sample infected file (limited to 1 MB); upload the ransom note; or enter the e-mail, URL, Onion, or/and Bitcoin address shown in the random demand to determine the ransomware type.

- **VirusTotal** (`https://www.virustotal.com/gui/home/upload`): This is a popular service for analyzing suspicious files for malware. You can use this service to either upload a file (with a maximum size of 550 MB) to examine it or type a URL to scan it for malware. VirusTotal also supports searching by IP address, domain, and file hash.

Popular Ransomware Removal Tools

Now that you know the type of ransomware that infects your system, let's continue to the next step to see whether there is a decryptor/unlocker for this type of ransomware.

As you already know, there are two types of ransomware; one locks the victim's computer screen, and the other type encrypts the victim's data. Let's start with the screen locker ransomware type.

Tools for Screen-Locking Ransomware

Screen-locking ransomware can be removed either by using a tool or manually. The following sections cover both methods.

Trend Micro Ransomware Screen Unlocker Tool

To get rid of screen-locking ransomware, you can use the Trend Micro Ransomware Screen Unlocker Tool. Please note that to use this tool, you need to install it on Windows while running in Safe Mode with Networking. If you do not know how to launch Windows in Safe Mode, check the following guide from NeoSmart: "How to boot into Safe Mode in Windows 10, 8, 7, Vista, and XP" (`https://neosmart.net/wiki/safe-mode`).

If the screen-locking ransomware is blocking Safe Mode with Networking, then you can still use this tool, but you need to use another version that runs from a USB device to unlock the infected machine. Both versions and usage guides can be found at `https://esupport.trendmicro.com/en-us/home/pages/technical-support/1105975.aspx`.

Manual Removal

You can try to manually remove the screen-locking ransomware by restarting your Windows PC in Safe Mode. This mode allows only trusted applications and services to start. Now install an anti-malware produce or update the installed one, and conduct a full scan to get rid of the ransomware.

You can also try to restore your OS to a previous state using the Windows System Restore feature. If you do not know how to restore your Windows computer, How-To Geek has a guide for this at `https://www.howtogeek.com/howto/windows-vista/using-windows-vista-system-restore`.

Encryption Ransomware Decryptors

This section provides information about downloading and using various file decryptor tools for different ransomware families.

- **No More Ransom** (`https://www.nomoreransom.org/en/decryption-tools.html`): This tool has decryptor tools for the following ransomware types: 777, AES_NI, Agent.iih, Alcatraz, Alpha, Amnesia, Amnesia2, Annabelle, Aura, Aurora, AutoIt, AutoLocky, BTCWare, BadBlock, BarRax, Bart, BigBobRoss, Bitcryptor, CERBER V1, Chimera, Coinvault, Cry128, Cry9, CrySIS, Cryakl, Crybola, Crypt888, CryptON, CryptXXX V1, CryptXXX V2, CryptXXX V3, CryptXXX V4, CryptXXX V5, CryptoMix, Cryptokluchen, DXXD, Damage, Democry, Derialock, Dharma, EncrypTile, Everbe, FenixLocker, FilesLocker versions 1 and v2, Fury, GandCrab (V1, V4, V5, V5.1, and V5.2 versions), GetCrypt, Globe, Globe/Purge, Globe2, Globe3, GlobeImposter, Gomasom, HKCrypt, HiddenTear, InsaneCrypt, JSWorm 2.0, Jaff, Jigsaw, LECHIFFRE, LambdaLocker, Lamer, Linux.Encoder.1, Linux.Encoder.3, Lortok, MacRansom, Marlboro, Marsjoke aka Polyglot, MegaLocker, Merry X-Mas, MirCop, Mole, Nemucod, NemucodAES, Nmoreira, Noobcrypt, Ozozalocker, PHP ransomware, Pewcrypt, Philadelphia, Planetary, Pletor, Popcorn, Pylocky, Rakhni, Rannoh, Rotor, SNSLocker, Shade, Simplocker, Stampado, Teamxrat/Xpan, TeslaCrypt V1, TeslaCrypt V2, TeslaCrypt V3, TeslaCrypt V4 Thanatos, Trustezeb, Wildfire, XData, XORBAT, XORIST, and ZQ. This web site offers a how-to guide for each listed ransomware decryptor to inform the user how to safely remove the infection from their machine. No More Ransom is an important site (it is an initiative by the National High-Tech Crime Unit of the Netherlands' police, Europol's European Cybercrime Centre, and McAfee) that can identify the type of ransomware in addition to offering a decryptor if there is one available. Always begin your search for a ransomware decryptor at the No More Ransom site.

- **Quickheal Free Ransomware Decryption Tool** (`https://www.quickheal.com/free-ransomware-decryption-tool`): This tool decrypts 19 types of encryption ransomware.

- **No Ransom From Kaspersky** (https://noransom.kaspersky.com): This site has decryptors for the following ransomware types: Rakhni, Agent.iih, Aura, Autoit, Pletor, Rotor, Lamer, Cryptokluchen, Lortok, Democry, Bitman (TeslaCrypt) versions 3 and 4, Chimera, Crysis (versions 2 and 3), Jaff, Dharma and new versions of the Cryakl ransomware, Rannoh, AutoIt, Fury, Cryakl, Crybola, CryptXXX (versions 1, 2, and 3), Polyglot aka Marsjoke, Shade versions 1 and 2, CoinVault and Bitcryptor, Wildfire, Xorist, and Vandev.

- **Avast** (https://www.avast.com/ransomware-decryption-tools): This site has free ransomware decryption tools for the following ransomware types: AES_NI, Alcatraz Locker, Apocalypse, BadBlock, Bart, BigBobRoss, BTCWare, Crypt888, CryptoMix (Offline), CrySiS, EncrypTile, FindZip, GandCrab, Globe, HiddenTear, Jigsaw, LambdaLocker, Legion, NoobCrypt, Stampado, SZFLocker, TeslaCrypt, and XData.

- **Emsisoft** (https://www.emsisoft.com/decrypter): This site has free decryptor tools for the following ransomware types: GetCrypt, JSWorm 2.0, MegaLocker, ZQ Ransomware, CryptoPokemon, Planetary, Aurora, HKCrypt (also known as Hacked Ransomware), PewCrypt, BigBobRoss, NemucodAES, Amnesia2, Amnesia, Cry128, Cry9, Damage, CryptON aka Nemesis aka X3M, MRCR or Merry X-Mas, Marlboro, Globe3, Globe2, Globe, OpenToDecrypt, GlobeImposter, NMoreira, OzozaLocker, Al-Namrood, FenixLocker, Fabiansomware, Philadelphia, Stampado, ApocalypseVM, Apocalypse, BadBlock, Xorist, 777, AutoLocky, Nemucod, DMALocker2, HydraCrypt, DMALocker, CrypBoss, Gomasom, LeChiffre, KeyBTC, Radamant, CryptInfinite, PClock, CryptoDefense, and Harasom.

- **McAfee Ransomware Recover** (https://www.mcafee.com/enterprise/en-us/downloads/free-tools/ransomware-decryption.html): Also called Mr2, this is a packed decryptor for different types of ransomware.

- **Trend Micro Ransomware File Decryptor** (`https://esupport.trendmicro.com/en-us/home/pages/technical-support/1114221.aspx`): This site decrypts files of the following ransomware families: (CryptXXX V1, V2, V3), (CryptXXX V4, V5), TeslaCrypt V1, TeslaCrypt V2, TeslaCrypt V3, TeslaCrypt V4, SNSLocker, AutoLocky, BadBlock, 777, XORIST, XORBAT, CERBER V1, Stampado, Nemucod, Chimera, LECHIFFRE, MirCop, Jigsaw, Globe/Purge, DXXD, Teamxrat/Xpan, Crysis, TeleCrypt, DemoTool, and WannaCry (WCry).

- **KnowBe4** (`https://blog.knowbe4.com/are-there-free-ransomware-decryptors`): This lists 100+ free ransomware decryption tools.

- **Avg** (`https://www.avg.com/en-ww/ransomware-decryption-tools`): This site has ransomware decryption tools for the following ransomware forms: Apocalypse, BadBlock, Bart, Crypt888, Legion, SZFLocker, and TeslaCrypt.

Warning!   After getting infected with ransomware, inexperienced users may start their computer in Safe Mode and perform a full antivirus scan to remove the ransomware. By doing this, they will remove the ransomware from their machine, but the infected files will still be encrypted. The problem here is that they will lose the ability to pay the ransom. Do this only if you are determined not to pay the ransom.

Note!   If you cannot find a decryptor for the ransomware infecting your computer, then try to search the Internet using Google. For example, if the extension of your files got changed after infection into a `.Codnat` extension, then search for *remove codnat ransomware.*

You can search for the latest ransomware decryptors on Twitter by typing the following in the search box: **#ransomware decryptor since:2019-06-14**. (The date section in the example is the start date and can be changed to get the latest tweets about ransomware decryptors.)

Recover Deleted Files

The majority of encryption ransomware families work by encrypting a copy of the victim's files first and then deleting the original version. There are many tools for file recovery, and many of them offer a free version with limited features. If your files are important and the ransomware performs a kind of secure deletion of original files, do not despair. Seek help from a professional digital forensics examiner. The investigation techniques employed by digital forensics examiners can recover deleted files even though they have been deleted securely (overwritten) by the attacking ransomware.

Here is a list of some popular data recovery software. If you want to buy a commercial solution, make sure to buy the one that supports different storage devices like external hard disks, USB drives, SD cards, and fixed hard drives.

- **TestDisk and PhotoRec** (`https://www.cgsecurity.org/wiki/TestDisk_Download`): This is open source software that works on Windows, Linux, and macOS.

- **Undelete 360** (`http://www.undelete360.com`): This is freeware with no limitation for the size of data recovery.

- **EaseUS Data Recovery Wizard Free** (`https://www.easeus.com/datarecoverywizard/free-data-recovery-software.htm`): This can recover up to 2 GB for free.

- **MiniTool Power Data Recovery Free** (`https://www.minitool.com/data-recovery-software/free-for-windows.html`): The free version is limited to recovering 1 GB of data.

- **Disk Drill** (`https://www.cleverfiles.com/disk-drill-windows.html`): The free version is limited to recovering 500 MB of data.

- **Recuva** (`http://www.ccleaner.com/recuva`): This is freeware for Windows.

- **SoftPerfect File Recovery** (`https://www.softperfect.com/products/filerecovery`): This is a freeware tool.

Warning!   When recovering deleted files, make sure to recover them onto a portable hard drive. Do not restore them to the same drive that you are recovering data from, as you might overwrite these files and lose them forever.

If you use any of the previous tools and are still unable to recover some—or even all—of your data, then do not panic. Seek help from professional digital forensics examiner to investigate the infected drive and check for the possibility of data recovery.

Note!   The topic of digital forensics has become integrated into all computer security domains. If you are a newcomer to this field and want to understand how digital forensics techniques can be used to investigate ransomware attacks and recover deleted files, then I advise you to grab my book *Digital Forensics Basics* (Apress, 2019).

Resources for Tracking Ransomware

I have already listed different combat techniques to prevent ransomware infection; however, new attack methods are being developed daily, so no one can know all the attack vectors coming in the future. That's why organizations must have some insight into what is happening in general in the ransomware arena. This *cyber-threat intelligence* provides actionable information about threat actors and early warning signs of ransomware attacks, allowing organizations to strength their cyber defenses against all critical attack vectors.

Having a reliable and current source of cyber-threat information will help security teams to respond more efficiently to a ransomware attack and to find the required information more quickly. Some organizations are even incorporating cyber-threat intelligence feeds into their network directly so they can immediately react to emerging threats.

Various organizations offer cyber-threat intelligence feeds. The following are the most popular ones:

- **Malware traffic analysis** (`http://malware-traffic-analysis.net/2019/index.html`): This has been monitoring malicious network traffic since 2013.

- **APT Groups and Operations** (`https://docs.google.com/spreadsheets/u/1/d/1H9_xaxQHpWaa4O_Son4GxOYOIzlcBWMsdvePFX68EKU/pubhtml`): This covers advanced persistent threat (APT) activity.

- **Automated Indicator Sharing (AIS)** (`https://www.dhs.gov/cisa/automated-indicator-sharing-ais`): This is managed by the Department of Homeland Security (DHS); it facilitates the exchange of cyber-threat indicators between the federal government and the private sector.

- **FireHOL** (`https://iplists.firehol.org`): This analyzes various security feeds related to online attacks such as malicious IP addresses, malware, botnets, command-and-control servers, and more.

- **IBM X-Force Exchange** (`https://exchange.xforce.ibmcloud.com`): This lists the latest global security risks.

- **MalwareINT** (`https://intel.malwaretech.com`): This shows a world map displaying the geographical distribution of malware infection and new botnets.

- **SANS Institute Internet Storm Center** (`https://isc.sans.edu`): This provides data on various emerging cyber threats.

- **Botvrij** (`http://www.botvrij.eu`): This free service provides different data sets of open source indicators of compromise that you can use in your security devices to alert about the possible malicious activity.

- **C&C Tracker** (`http://osint.bambenekconsulting.com/feeds/c2-ipmasterlist.txt`): This provides an updated list of command-and-control IP addresses.

- **Cyber Cure free intelligence feeds** (`https://www.cybercure.ai`): This provides free to use cyber-intelligence feeds by collecting different security indicators from commercial vendors running honeypots and honeynets.

- **Threatfeeds** (`https://threatfeeds.io`): This service provides free and open source threat intelligence feeds.

Note!   Business organizations can also use information collected through information sharing and analysis centers (ISACs). These are nonprofit organizations specializing in gathering intelligence about different cyber threats and suggesting prevention and best practices to counter such threats. ISACs also foster the sharing of gathered information between the public and private sectors.

The European Union Agency for Cybersecurity (ENISA) has published a study about ISACs in Europe. You can download it from `https://www.enisa.europa.eu/ publications/information-sharing-and-analysis-center-isacs- cooperative-models`. To find a list of ISACs grouped by industry in the Unites States, go to `https://www.nationalisacs.org`.

Here are some other useful web sites for getting information about ransomware attack vectors and mitigation strategies:

- **US-CERT** (`https://www.us-cert.gov/ncas/tips/ST19-001`): This is a security tip (ST19-001) called "Protecting Against Ransomware."

- **FireEye** (`https://www.fireeye.com/blog/threat-research. html/category/etc/tags/fireeye-blog-tags/ransomware`): This contains threat research about ransomware.

- **Emsisoft** (`https://blog.emsisoft.com/en/category/protection- guides/spotlight-ransomware`): This is a multipart series covering all aspects of ransomware, from infection vectors, encryption, and payment to the best way to remove ransomware once on the system.

- **knowbe4** (`https://info.knowbe4.com/ransomware-hostage- rescue-manual-0`): This is the Ransomware Hostage Rescue Manual.

Summary

Ransomware decryption tools allow you to recover files encrypted with ransomware without paying the ransom. There is no general decryptor for all ransomware infections, as each ransomware variant requires its own decryptor. Ransomware decryptors are easy to use by casual users, and most of them come free. However, some types require the user to have some technical skills to decrypt infected files.

As ransomware attacks become more prevalent and have significant legal and financial risks to both individuals and organizations, the need for a ransomware response plan is crucial for any organization that wants to know what to do in the event of a successful ransomware attack; this is the subject of the next and last chapter of this book.

CHAPTER 9

Responding to Ransomware Attacks

Creating a Ransomware Incident Response Plan

Driven by easier access and greater financial payoff, the number of ransomware attacks is expected to intensify in the future. Criminals are now focusing their efforts on targeting high-profile organizations, government entities, educational institutions, and healthcare organizations, and they will continue these attacks because of the ability to be fully anonymous when receiving ransoms and because the high success rate achieved by targeting large organizations for a bigger payout.

An *incident response plan* is a set of instructions used by the IT staff in organizations to mitigate, detect, respond to, and recover from cybersecurity incidents. The ultimate purpose of an incident response plan is to prevent any damage to IT systems that may lead to a data breach or service disruption.

The team responsible for implementing an incident response plan is called the *computer security incident response team* (CSIRT). The CSIRT is composed of IT professionals with formal IT security training who are responsible for coordinating all efforts of handling cybersecurity incidents, beginning from communicating with different parties inside an organization and containing the damage, through recovering from security incidents, to communicating with external parties such as the press, law enforcement, and other affected parties such as stakeholders and customers.

In this chapter, I discuss the main elements of a ransomware incident response plan and see how the existence of such a plan can greatly help in minimizing ransomware damage and recovering normal operations quickly.

© Nihad A. Hassan 2019
N. A. Hassan, *Ransomware Revealed*, https://doi.org/10.1007/978-1-4842-4255-1_9

Ransomware Incident Lifecycle

While you can have a general ransomware incident response plan that fits most situations, the specific details will vary according to the type of system involved in the incident. In this section, I talk about how to respond to ransomware incidents using recommendations based on the incident response lifecycle (see Figure 9-1), as described in the National Institute of Standards and Technology (NIST) Computer Security Incident Handling Guide.[1]

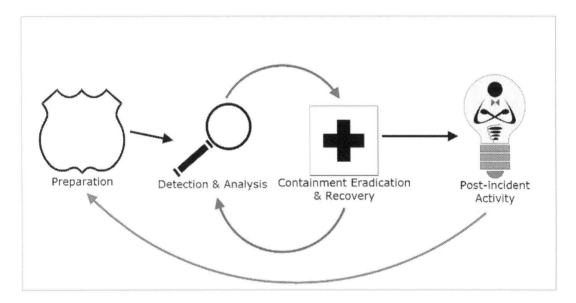

Figure 9-1. *Incident response life cycle, adopted from NIST's Computer Security Incident Handling Guide*

Preparation

The elements of the preparation phase were covered in detail in Part II of this book. In preparation, an organization describes the steps and countermeasures that must be implemented to secure its working environment (network, applications, IT systems, and human aspect) from ransomware attacks. This phase is considered the most important one as it mainly describes the mitigation steps that must be implemented to

---

[1] The National Institute of Standards and Technology, "Computer Security Incident Handling Guide" July 2, 2019 https://nvlpubs.nist.gov/nistpubs/SpecialPublications/NIST.SP.800-61r2.pdf

prevent a ransomware or malware attack from taking place. Ransomware technology is evolving rapidly, and having a robust multilayered defense strategy can halt an attack before it can access your environment.

Although the preparation phase is managed by a different team than the CSIRT and is implemented before the incident takes place, NIST insists on the importance of this phase and recommends it as the first phase of any incident response plan, because of its essential role in the success of all kinds of security incident response programs.

The following recommendations should be covered in the preparation phase of any ransomware incident response plan (each one has been covered in detail in the previous chapters):

- **Security awareness training**: End-user security training helps prevent ransomware attacks by making users aware of how malicious actors can penetrate and infect IT systems (e.g., users should understand how e-mail phishing attacks work). Understanding the anatomy of a ransomware attack should be incorporated into any security awareness training program so employees can report ransomware incidents once discovered to prevent ransomware from propagating the infection to other devices within the target network.

- **Endpoint devices defense**: A company should harden endpoint computers and mobile devices (e.g., stopping unnecessary services and protocols, closing unused ports, and so on). This also includes installing antivirus and anti-malware solutions, keeping the OS and applications current, governing running executables on endpoints, and performing other countermeasures help to make your computing device more resilient to ransomware and other malware infections.

- **Network defense**: A company should secure the entry points to the network through intrusion prevention systems (IPSs)/intrusion detection systems (IDSs) and firewalls, implement network segmentation to isolate infected networks more easily, use least privilege access, enforce strong authentication, install anti-spam solutions on e-mail servers, scan all incoming/outgoing e-mail attachments, enforce application whitelisting across the organization network, and enforce physical security measures; these are among the things you can do to secure the network environment.

- **Security policies**: You must have an up-to-date security policy and make sure it is enforced on all users who are accessing organization IT assets and resources.

- **Incident response plan**: Every organization should have a clear and up-to-date incident response plan that defines the roles and responsibilities of each employee once a cyber-attack incident (e.g., ransomware attack) is detected.

Tip!   An incident response plan should be accompanied by a disaster recovery plan to restore normal operations quickly and to comply with many official regulations (e.g., HIPAA).

Detection and Analysis

Ransomware incidents can be detected via different means. If you come across any of the following signs on your computing device, then there is a high probability that you are a victim of a ransomware attack:

- A splash screen covers the whole screen and blocks access to the infected device.

- You find encrypted files on your drive or files with strange extensions that you cannot open.

- The desktop wallpaper has been replaced with a ransom note (see Figure 9-2).

- You find text/HTML files that contain ransom payment instructions in every folder that contains data that has been encrypted by the ransomware.

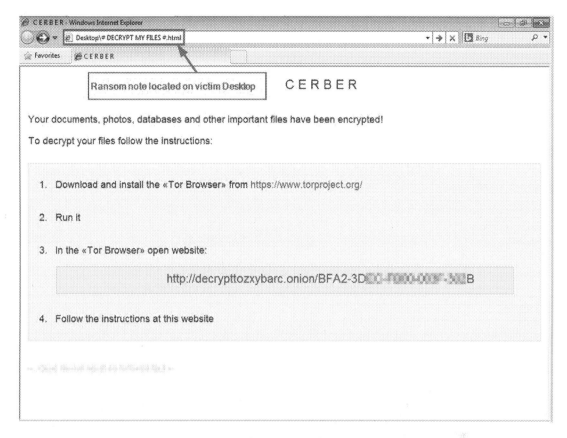

Figure 9-2. *CERBER ransom note (HTML file) located on victim's desktop*

Warning!   Sometimes a user may discover a ransomware attack while it is still encrypting files and before displaying the ransom note. For example, when a user tries to open a file and finds it inaccessible and with a strange file extension, then there is a high probability that there is a ransomware attack underway. In that case, the user should shut down the computer immediately and seek help from the IT security staff.

In the analysis phase, you are concerned with answering the following two questions:

- What type of ransomware is infecting your system?

- How did the ransomware get into your system (what is the infection vector)?

I covered in Chapter 2 how to identify the type of ransomware using free online services. Chapter 3 discussed in some detail the different ransomware families and main characteristics of each strain. Identifying the ransomware variant is essential to planning the later containment steps. For example, some ransomware variants have propagation capabilities, while others don't.

For the second question, as discussed in Chapter 2, ransomware can be introduced into an organization using different attack vectors. The most common ones are as follows:

- E-mail attachments and embedded malicious links

- Web browser vulnerabilities

- Pirated software (infected programs) bundled with malware

- Portable USB devices

Note!   The analysis of how ransomware was introduced to an organization environment can be postponed until the post-incident activity phase. However, it must be identified before doing the recovery to avoid infecting your files again.

Containment, Eradication, and Recovery

This phase contains three subphases.

Containment

After you have identified that your system has been infected with ransomware, you should follow these steps:

1. Isolate the infected system from the network. This can be accomplished by unplugging the network cable and/or disconnecting any wireless connectivity that may be in use to prevent spreading the infection to other devices across the network.

2. Acquire a memory dump of the infected machine. This can be helpful later to find the correct attack vector and to capture some information about the cryptographic routine used by the attackers, which can help in decrypting infected data.

(Many ransomware variants suffer from logical and programming errors when implementing the encryption routine, and this can be used by cryptographic experts to develop a general decryptor for it.)

3. Alternatively, if you cannot get a snapshot of RAM immediately, you can hibernate the infected machine and then seek help from a professional forensics examiner to capture the system memory for further investigation.

4. Secure your backup data or systems by taking them offline immediately. Perform a full scan to make sure the backup data is free from malware.

5. Disable shared drives.

6. Limit Internet connectivity from critical servers until discovering and eradicating the source of infection.

7. Now you need to determine the scope of the infection to see the actual damage caused by the ransomware. Check the following locations for signs of damage:

    •   Mapped shared drives.

    •   Mapped shared folders.

    •   All network storage devices. You do not need to shut down the file storage server. Instead, just terminate access to file shares using, for example, a firewall.

    •   Check all USB-connected devices such as external hard drives, USB sticks, SD cards, smartphones, tablets, laptops, and digital cameras.

    •   Check connected accounts on cloud storage (e.g., Dropbox, Google Drive).

8. Contact law enforcement immediately. If the incident took place in the United States, it is advisable to contact the nearest FBI office to report the ransomware and seek help.

Eradication

After the ransomware infection has been contained, you need to eradicate the ransomware from the infected machines. Eradication depends to a large extent on the attack vector that caused the ransomware infection. For example, if the ransomware enters your environment through an e-mail attachment, you should immediately purge all received e-mails in e-mail server and prevent all users from opening any e-mail with an attachment until you identify the malicious e-mail. You should also consider isolating any system, or even the entire network segment, where the suspicious e-mail has been opened until you verify that there is no ransomware infection in that area.

If the attack vector was introduced via a web browser (e.g., using an exploit kit), then you should consider blocking access to malicious web sites and performing a scan on the infected endpoints to update or remove all the components (e.g., vulnerable web browser add-ons and any outdated applications) used to carry the infection.

Note!   It is also advisable to change the passwords (for online accounts, operating systems, and network access) of all users who were affected by the ransomware attack.

Recovery

Now that the type of ransomware and the root cause of the infection have been identified clearly, the recovery process begins. You have four possible responses to select from.

Restore from Backup

This is the most feasible solution to fight against ransomware; however, it requires the existence of a good backup solution. Before proceeding with this option, ask yourself the following questions:

- Do you have a full backup for all affected machines?

- How often does your backup run (e.g., every week, every day, every hour)?

- Did you test your backup to make sure it is reliable and will work as expected?

- Is your backup data/system isolated from local endpoint devices to prevent propagating the infection to it?

If you have good answers for the previous questions, then you can rest assure that you can restore your infected data from the backup.

Note!   The backup system can be either an in-house or cloud backup solution.

Try Using a Decryptor

As covered earlier in the book, after knowing the ransomware family, conduct an online search to see whether there is a decryptor for that type of ransomware. Begin with the No More Ransom project (`https://www.nomoreransom.org`) and NJ Cybersecurity & Communications Integration Cell (`https://www.cyber.nj.gov/threat-profiles/ ransomware`). Currently, the NJCCIC profiles a total of 216 ransomware variants, and 97 of them have decryption tools or other technical solutions to use to recover your data.

Warning!   Make sure to attach all removable storage devices such as USB sticks and external hard drives that contain encrypted data before executing the decryptor to make sure their data will get decrypted as well.

Pay the Ransom

This option should be considered carefully, as covered in Chapter 7. Make sure to conduct a value assessment of the infected data to determine its importance to your business. You should also calculate any downtime costs associated with the attack.

Do Nothing!

Wipe clean infected systems and install a fresh OS and applications. Make sure to have a backup of the infected (encrypted) data in case someone develops a decryptor in the future.

Post-Incident Activity

After removing the ransomware infection and restoring normal operations, an organization should review the lessons learned from the attack to help prevent similar attacks from happening in the future. The following are the areas that should be reviewed for potential improvement:

- Implement defense technology solutions on both the endpoints and the network

- Enforce security policies

- Improve any shortcut in the end users' cybersecurity training to make them able to react appropriately to a ransomware attack

Finally, you need to implement the mitigation recommendations mentioned in this book to become more prepared and prevent future ransomware attacks.

Summary

Cyberattacks are inevitable, and ransomware threats are a significant threat to businesses and individuals alike. Each organization can respond to ransomware attacks differently. An organization response determines its ability to restore its operation quickly and to respond to different regulatory and legal claims imposed by such attacks.

Here is a brief summary of the key measures you should take in the case of a ransomware attack:

1. Isolate the infected system and secure the backup data.

2. Initiate a business continuity plan to restore operations quickly.

3. Seek help from a digital forensics examiner to preserve the evidence (e.g., network and server logs, system memory snapshots, endpoint device security logs, and so on) in a forensically sound manner.

4. Activate the incident response plan.

5. Document the incident and be prepared for any legal, insurance, or dispute claim.

Successful organizations learn from every security incident; they collect feedback, review implemented security controls (both technical and policies), and update their incident response plan and mitigation procedures accordingly to stay current with the latest threats imposed by ransomware and other malware types.

Index

© Nihad A. Hassan 2019
N. A. Hassan, *Ransomware Revealed*, https://doi.org/10.1007/978-1-4842-4255-1

Printed in the United States
By Bookmasters